Dame Eugenia

– Unedited

Alex Bruno

Dame Eugenia
– Unedited

The Last Official Full-length Interview

with **Dame Mary Eugenia Charles**

Dominica Political Leadership Legacy Series (DPLLS)
Book 1

Foreword: **Gordon Henderson**

Manuscriptology: **Nicole Georges-Bennett**

Copyright © 2023 Alex Bruno

Publisher: EXCELTIX LLC.
2500 Quantum Lakes Drive, Suite 203
Boynton Beach, Fl. 33426

Edition: First Printing

All rights Reserved. No part of this publication may be reproduced, distributed, or transmitted in any form or by any means without the prior written permission of the publisher. Except in the case of brief quotations embodied in critical reviews and certain other noncommercial uses permitted by copyright law.

ISBN: 978-0-9915728-0-9

Credits

Cover Design: Alex Bruno

Cover Art: E. T. Evelyn

Manuscriptology: Nicole Georges-Bennett

Transcription: Tamisha Toussaint and Alex Bruno

Consultative Oversight: Anaya Bruno

Book Design: Sam George

Disclaimer

This book, in great parts, represents the views of Dame Mary Eugenia Charles – in her own words. The author's contribution(s) are based on his interactions with Ms. Charles, and his own professional analysis of her narratives.

It is hoped that each reader takes away what he or she finds from this book, and it duly noted that no part of the text is designed to defame, glorify, contradict or replace what has already been know and or established about the deceased, former Honourable Prime Minister of Dominica, Dame Mary Eugenia Charles. Hopefully, typos and formatting errors discovered in the book will be graciously understood and forgiven.

Dedication

This book is dedicated to Garvin Bruno, my first child.

Table of contents

Epigraph	i
Preface	ii
Foreword	iv
About Dominica Political Leadership Legacy Series (DPLLS)	vii
Introduction	x
About the Dame	xv
Interview Begins (Tape #1)	1
Interview Continues (Tape #2)	94
Conclusion	181
Remembering the Dame	188
Afterword	194
Postscript	199
Acknowledgment	201
About the author	202
Explanatory Notes	206

Epigraph

"I changed some things in Dominica that required changing, and I intend, until I die, to keep on making sure that there are changes in Dominica for the benefit of Dominicans on a whole"

Dame Eugenia Charles

Preface

A frank and free-flowing discussion with one of the Caribbean's most recognizable political figures, Dame Mary Eugenia Charles of Dominica. What was certainly my most compelling media moment is now a treasure to the world of political leadership, and a welcome addition to Dominica's political history. Read through the text as you listen to the commanding voice of the Dame in this last full-length interview with the Caribbean's Iron Lady. This book is an unedited transcription of an exclusive one-on-one interview with Dame Mary Eugenia Charles. The interview was recorded on Tuesday 30th December 1999 at her residence in Roseau, Dominica.

The book is being released in recognition of Eugenia's life, her contributions to Dominica and as a tribute to those who have tried to share knowledge against all odds. This publication, the first in a series of Dominica Political Leadership Legacy Series (DPLLS), sets the tone for what I hope will be a new trend of political engagement in Dominican politics. The DPLLS is an original thought which I felt should be expressed in the form of responsible research. The series examines the life, work and times of all elected political leaders: Prime Ministers, Premiere(s), Chief Minister(s) of Dominica.

The project aims to establish aspects of the leaders' contributions to the administration of the nation that can be seen as their lasting legacies.

Foreword

I have had the pleasure of knowing Alex Bruno for many years, though it wasn't until recently that I discovered that his given name, 'Alex,' is actually short for Alexander. Yet, regardless of the name he goes by, his life has been one of remarkable accomplishments that are truly worthy of an autobiography.

Over the years, I have watched Alex excel in a variety of fields. He has been an executive for a small airline company, a radio personality and journalist, a master of ceremonies, a songwriter, a singer, a playwright, a concert producer, and a blogger. I was surprised to learn that he also spent time, a tiny bit, in law enforcement, a testament to his diverse range of experiences.

Today, Alex Bruno is a respected lecturer at a prestigious US college, where he imparts his knowledge and insight to eager students. While some may argue that his true calling lies in the field of politics, Alex's training as a political scientist has certainly served him well in all of his endeavors. Bruno loves research, and his personal archives contain interviews with numerous state leaders. I have always been hopeful that these would one day be published as books. That day has come.

This book is a commencement of the process, and having read the manuscript. I attest that readers are in for an engagement which is probably unlike any other that I have personally experienced. It is simply fascinating to hear the views of Eugenia Charles in her own words. I believe that it is quite intriguing for Alex to release this exclusive interview with Mary Eugenia Charles, a quarter century after it was recorded. This release is certainly worth the wait. It is, in some sense, a celebration of Alex Bruno's expertise, training, and experience as an academic and political practitioner.

The book provides invaluable insights into the socio-economic, political, and historical context of Dominica, as seen through the words of one of the Caribbean's most celebrated leaders. This book is strongly recommended for the general population of Dominica, as it sheds light on the country's past, it informs the present and could even impact the future. Moreover, this publication marks the beginning of a series that will showcase every leader of Dominica, including, and especially, Patrick John, the first Prime Minister. *Dame Eugenia – Unedited* is an essential read for anyone interested in the history, government, development and the politics of Dominica, and any island nation I dare say.

Let me state that the depth and breadth of Alex's accomplishments are truly extraordinary, and I am honored to have known him for so long.

Gordon Henderson

Dominica Political Leadership Legacy Series (DPLLS)

The Dominica Political Leadership Legacy Series (DPLLS) is a 10-year project, in the first instance (August 2023 – August 2033). The idea is driven by a thirst for political knowledge and improved, cordial, respectful, responsible and progressive engagements within the Dominican political space.

The average Dominican is not as politically predisposed as would be desired, and because this has created a widening divide among the citizenry, particularly over the last two decades, this new thrust will hopefully address some of the nuances which have contributed to the disparities in Dominican politics. In order for there to be political growth, people should engage, but there is a natural spirit of disengagement and intolerance which have gripped too many.

If and when we learn about each other's ways, then - and only then - will we see meaningful progress. We do better when we understand each other, but political partisanship has not allowed this to happen. DPLLS intends to promote a different type of political mobility.

It is the view of this DPLLS project, that there should be a decade dedicated to begin the redefinition of Dominica's political culture. By tracing the political chain back to Edward Oliver Leblanc, and looking at the journey of Dominica's political leadership in-between to the contemporary. DPLLS is indeed taking a meaningful and apolitical dive into a space which has not been truthfully analyzed from an impartial and frank point of view. Over the next decade, we will examine the political activities and attempts at leadership of the same.

It is our hope that a new cadre of political leaders will emerge from the exercise, and that the next phase of DPLLS will include practical and hands-on activities which speak to growth and prosperity among Dominicans. In that case, DPLLS will not simply present analysis of past and current political leaders, instead, we will engage newer and younger aspiring leaders – current leaders as well – by conducting workshops, hosting seminars, presenting lectures, staging debates, promoting and hosting panel discussions, we will offer coaching in political leadership skills, mentor students into becoming better citizens, promote media relations and public sensitivity around civic engagement, and focus our attention on the empowerment of mainly the next generation of Dominican youth.

DPLLS is an Alex Bruno initiative in partnership with EXCELTIX LLC., Gohen Music, Caribbean Agency for Political Advancement (CAPA), G & D Enterprises Inc., with collaboration from the University of the West Indies (UWI), Fort Young Hotel, The Dominica Calypso 'Kaiso' Hall of Fame (DCKHF), The Sign Man and One Caribbean Culture (OCC).

Introduction

I remember, in September 1996, when Dennis Joseph invited me to accompany him as he switched jobs from Island Communications Services (Kairi FM) to manage the Dominica Broadcasting Services (DBS Radio). Without hesitation, I said yes! After all, it was my dream employment, to become a National Broadcaster and a member of the DBS family.

I grabbed the opportunity especially as I had been previously overlooked for employment by Charles James, the station's General Manager at the time, who Insisted that I did not have the necessary qualifications. I, of course, volunteered at DBS for some time between my stint at Voice of the Island Radio (VOI) and Kairi FM between 1993 and 1994. I kept a steady presence, and kept knocking at the door of my opportunity.

The moment had arrived, and I moved to DBS. Guided by the general manager, Mr. Dennis Joseph, I created, produced, hosted and presented a once weekly radio program called Positively Dominica. Positively Dominica began airing in 1997 and was inspired by divine intervention, when my deceased great grandmother who visited me in a dream, beseeched me to do something good with the opportunity that was presented to me in my new role as a broadcaster. I remember this as if it were yesterday, and I obliged. Mama, my great grandmother, had already been gone for sixteen years by then, but she somehow kept her presence in my life through spiritual connection. I would get this sense that she was always in my presence especially through my adversities. Two and a half decades later, here comes the release of this never before presented body of work which was expected to be part of my Positively Dominica feature.

My discussion with Dame Eugenia came around the same time that One Hundred Great began airing on DBS Radio. In fact, the interview was recorded for that program. This program followed-on from Positively Dominica. It was the eve of a new decade, and partisan politics permeated the Dominican social atmosphere. It was this atmosphere which occasioned the change, or augmentation to the Positively Dominica feature.

I remember as if it were yesterday. Dennis and I sat in his office to discuss the details of the program. He said that it was more or less be a positive type of feature, and that it would be prerecorded and saved for posterity. I had recently taken on a new contract to operate as Special Projects Assistance, and this program was one of my special responsibilities.

I was also asked to produce a five-minute prime time, Positively Dominica spot for airing at 7:00 am, Monday to Friday on DBS Radio. I did and was politically branded for this because the opposition Dominica Labour Party (DLP) did not see the sense in introducing such a program on the eve of a General Election. I did not understand the big hullabaloo then, but I do now. Anyway, the program went on and it was the turn of Dame Eugenia. She was adamant about not being featured on any program, idea, thing, forum, panel, organization and the like, with Patrick John, the former and first Prime Minister of Dominica. I remember the Dame telling me directly, that, "if Patrick John is a great individual, I am not one and never want to be one."

I took her refusals for an interview in strides and after months of steady begging, the Dame granted me an interview. She however insisted that: "I am not in anything with Patrick John; I am not going to give clearance to have this aired along with anything having to do with Patrick John."

I was confused, because after agreeing to the interview, the Dame demanded that I could not use it for the purpose for which it was intended. I could not release it as a feature of 100 Great Dominicans. I did the interview, anyway, not knowing how, when or where I would present it. I gazed at the cassettes for years before deciding to do something about them. I transcribed the final word of this interview on Friday, December 24, 2021. Tamisha Toussaint did the lion's share of the transcription, however, as part of her duties when she was employed as the Administrative Assistant of my media and communications company - PAWOL. Because of my inefficiency as a typist. I had the privilege of listening to the interview several hundred times throughout the transcribing process. It took me several years to finish, and at this point, I am totally immersed in the story of this iconic Dominican.

I present this work to the world with the very same fervor and passion that was placed into the project. I believe that the following passage which was written on Dame Eugenia by Dr. Lennox Honychurch will help prepare you for my conversation with her. This article puts my conversation with the Dame into context. Dr. Honychurch is not only Dominica's most noted historian; he actually had a front-row seat in the theatre of Dominica's politics during the 1970s and 80s.

As discussed in the interview, Dr. Honychurch served as a member of Dominica's delegation to England on the opposition side, so he is a fitting person to introduce the Dame. Honychurch also served as an Honorable Senator in the Dominican Legislature (House of Assembly of Dominica) between 1975 to 1979, and became Press

Secretary to The Government of Dominica for the first year of the Dominica Freedom Party's first term in office (1980 –1981).

About the Dame

Dame Mary Eugenia Charles, Prime Minister, lawyer, politician and journalist who died in Martinique on Tuesday 6 September 2005 was born May 15, 1919 at Pointe Michel village on the south-west coast of Dominica.

She was educated at the Convent High School, Roseau, and St. Joseph's Convent, Grenada. She read law at University of Toronto and was called to the Bar at the Inner Temple, London in 1949. She began private practice in Dominica that year. She wrote anonymous articles for the Herald and later the Star newspapers that were highly critical of the ruling Dominica Labour Party (DLP).

When the government reacted she was in the vanguard of those who founded the Dominica Freedom Party (DFP) in 1968 following demonstrations against the passing of Seditious and Undesirable Publications Act in July by the DLP, then under the premiership of E.O. LeBlanc. She failed to win the Roseau north seat in the general election of 1970 contesting against Patrick John, but entered the House of Assembly as a Nominated Member that year. In the general elections of 1975, she contested and won the

Roseau Central seat and became Leader of Opposition in the new parliament. She was a delegate at the constitutional Conference for independence held at Marlborough House, London in 1977 and was an active spokesperson in the public meetings related to the constitution in the run-up to independence in November 1978.

During political upheavals and a constitutional crisis in 1979 she served as a member of the Committee for National Salvation (CNS) that brokered the creation of an interim government to administer Dominica until general elections could be organized. She became the first Caribbean woman Prime Minister when she led the DFP to victory in the 1980 general elections. During this time, she was given the nickname 'Mamo', by which she was popularly known for the rest of her life.

Regionally she immediately became part a formidable team of Caribbean leaders including Edward Seaga of Jamaica and Tom Adams of Barbados who dominated Caribbean public life in the 1980s. Her first term was dedicated to reconstruction of housing, roads and other infrastructure destroyed by Hurricane David which had hit Dominica in August 1979, and in getting the business of government and foreign relations back into order.

This was made more difficult by destabilization and the attempted coups to overthrow her government in 1981 and the court cases that followed. Her government was re-elected in 1985 with a reduced majority and again in 1990 when the UWP, formed in 1988, became the main opposition in parliament. In 1991 she was knighted as Dame of the Order of Bath by Queen Elizabeth II at Harare, Zimbabwe during the Commonwealth Heads of Government Conference.

She retired from the House of Assembly in 1995 and her Dominica Freedom Party lost the general elections of that year after fifteen years in power. During that time the country rose to an economic peak in 1988 but the momentum was not maintained and by 1993 there was evidence of the beginning of an economic decline due mainly to changes in international trade affecting the banana industry, the reduction of foreign aided projects and the economics of scale in relation to small independent island states. Conflict over her domination of the cabinet and her views on a successor marred the last two years of her leadership.

Her firm and forthright character and clear cut opinions were seen by some to be abrasive and she made many enemies but her admirers cited these as the only means by which to accomplish results under difficult circumstances. Dame Eugenia was best known outside of Dominica for her staunch anti-communism during the last years of the Cold War in the Caribbean and, as Chairman of the OECS, for leading the invitation to the United States government under President Ronald Reagan to invade Grenada in October 1983. For this she was often referred to as 'The Iron Lady of the Caribbean'. Following her retirement in 1995 she watched from the sidelines as the fortunes of the Dominica Freedom Party rapidly declined under new leadership, eventually losing all of its seats in the House of Assembly at the general elections of 2005.

By then, Dame Eugenia's memory and mental capacity to absorb what was going on around her was fading and in the opinion to some close to her, she had lost the will to live by the time she fell and fractured her left hip on 27 August 2005 and was flown to Martinique for treatment. Her passing removes yet another of the giants of Caribbean leadership who were active in the latter part of the 20th century.

Dr. Lennox Honychurch

The Interview Begins

This long-withheld interview began following a brief pause, by me, to collect my composure and to whisper a few words to the Creator, from whom I sought the strength to deal with this very intimidating and indomitable iconic and truly historic figure – Dame, Mary Eugenia Charles.

Please allow me, however, to let you into the ambiance of my mind by walking you through the moments right before the interview actually began. After being invited, and ushered upstairs to Eugenia's dwelling by a female attendant, I walked into the spacious living room which gave a sense of welcome and calm; the sort of calm which was certainly not present on my short journey from DBS radio, and particularly on my excursion from the ground floor to the interviewing room, which took a flight of about 30 steps.

The journey from DBS' main studios on Victoria Street, a two minute drive to Dame Eugenia's house on Cork Street, Roseau, and the journey up the stairs took less than a minute. This however, felt like an eternity. I had never met the Dame before, so I did not know what to expect. But there she was, already seated and not quite as intimidating as I had feared.

She was wearing a brownish sleeveless dress with flowery dark prints, her silvery-white and slightly black hair was brushed backwards and left lose; she gave me a half smile and brief but firm steer, followed by a gentle handshake, after which she said "come take a seat."

I sat across from her, placing the recording device and spare tape on a table between us. I peeled the plastic covering from the cassettes, plugged in my mic, **took up position on the armless chair to the left side of an already seated Dame Eugenia - she was steering politely from about 2 – 3 feet away.** The room where the interview was to be conducted was properly lit with a blend of natural and artificial lighting.

The somber interior colors of the room blended with the atmosphere that the Dame had created. There was a corner table with educational articles, a newspaper and what appeared to be a notebook, and there might have been a lower shelf to that table. The table was placed to the left of the Dame and I. The roof of the room had no additional ceiling – the characteristic white ceiling which adorned my house and that of the neignbours in my village community of Calibishie.

There were a couple of wall hangings, and an open adjacent space – further left of the Dame and I; an area for slightly more entertaining social reception I suppose.

The area where Dame Eugenia and I sat appeared to be a den; somewhat like a conversation cockpit. The surrounding was clean, the space was quiet, and I had a view of the Dame and the wall which protected her from leaning back too far back. I informed her that I was ready to begin recording.

She replied, "sure!"

I pressed record and the conversation began…

Alex Bruno: Cork Street, Roseau. Dame Eugenia um, a lot of talks have been going around, um some that you might have heard about and many you might not have heard about, but we all know that you are one of the stalwarts in terms of Dominica's History. I'm very happy you decided to speak with us and I would like you, now, to set your record clear as to everything you would like documented about you as a, a very powerful – not just Dominican, but Caribbean and world figure. Good morning to you.

Dame Eugenia: Thank you a lot, because I mean, I don't consider myself famous. The persons elected me to do things for Dominicans, and so I did them; the things they wanted. But importantly, I think it's very important for leaders to realize that it is a job of the citizens, so you are really serving people. So, you must know what they want and you must be able to tell them why they can't have the things they want; I don't think you should be dishonest about it. I think you should be clearly, and tell them you can't have this because we do not have the money to do it and nobody gets to give us the money to do it. But look at, for instance this, this, this storm we had there which wasn't even a hurricane it wasn't declared a hurricane, but you know a lot of people on the coast lost, lost their property. Have you heard any comment from government on that? I haven't, maybe I have not been listening in at the right time. I know one comment I did hear is that they; somebody seems to have said that instead of talking about international airport, they should look and see which way they can help the people who suffered damage from this hurricane, and the

Prime Minister replied and said no matter what happened in the hurricane, he is going to go ahead with his plan they going to build the airport and so and so forth, so and so forth. I'm not against it, you have to know what's best for Dominica, and if he thinks the airport is going to bring all the goodies that Dominica requires, he has a right to go on with the idea. What I'm saying is that you also have to consider the persons who are suffering now as a result of the, of the… they didn't bring the sea damage, it came because a lot of people living by the sea. Are we going to change our style? Are we going to move further inland? What plans are we going to have to make sure that this doesn't happen every year?

Alex Bruno: Well, there might have been a few statements I believe especially in the Bay Town area,

I think people wouldn't be allowed to relocate there and in certain part of -

Dame Eugenia: They were never replaced anyway by the Bay Front because twice we have moved the people from the Bay Front and put them in houses right on top the hill, so it's only a temporary thing, and when people didn't have a place to go, we let them stay there for a while, but the idea was they were preparing to move into a place that was safer and they could do something more for themselves.

Alex Bruno: Dame, for the purpose of documenting the um, what we are doing I know you don't want me to call it one of the hundred greats I know you prefer me not to call it that but we are going to do a story on you and in order to document it in terms of perspective in history, why don't we start with your parents who they were and how you came about to be?

Dame Eugenia: First of all, my parents, you know, my father was a peasant. He was a small farmer he bought a small piece of land he worked it, he made money, he sold it got a bigger piece and went on like that in life, always, working his land selling it for a profit and buying a bigger piece and working it again and in that way, he gave a lot of other people work who worked with him. His father had been a peasant before him at the top of Point Mitchel he had a piece of land which he never had a car road to the road is so impossible; you would have to go by horseback to the sea to bathe their horses every morning. But as a result, you were brought up in a family which realized the virtue of work, that everybody had to work if you were going to get anywhere and that you owed it to yourself and to your country to work.

Alex Bruno: Your, your, you mention your father, JB, and his father; can you tell us their names and where they might have been from?

Dame Eugenia: My father's, my grandfather's name was François Charles. He was born in one of the French islands, he came here from the French island. His wife who was also French, and he married her when he was a slave, she was a slave at the time they got married and she got her freedom. In fact, her father… her husband paid for her freedom after a time so she became a free person. And in those days, you know when they freed the slaves, they often gave them a piece of land so they could continue to work on and you can look at some of the documents in the Registry and you will see this reference; with the fact that so and so was given his freedom and he was given his portion of land so he could sustain himself as result of being free, and so…and my father was um, was brought up - I think by pretty strict parents, and hardworking people in our family. We realized you don't get anywhere unless working hard, nobody owes you a living. You had to do things for yourself and you had to prepare to make sacrifices to get anywhere. My parents only had elementary school education, and yet there was never a time in our household when we didn't know that their ambition was that we should have university education. They weren't asking the Government for any help they were working themselves to pay for us to be trained at university, so all of us got professions.

Alex Bruno: So, your, your, your father consequently was born on a plantation; was he?

Dame Eugenia: Not a plantation, a small estate a 30 acres estate the heights of Point Mitchel they will never have a road to it - it is so difficult to get to, and we spent a lot of our time there. That's where our grandparents lived and then it went to my father who was the only son alive at the time he died; the land went to him and, my father- I was born at Point Mitchel village, that's where we all made our home and then my father worked the land. He should go up every morning walking up the mountain to plant coffee. Coffee was the thing that was important in his time and then when South America took over the coffee market, he went into limes and other things like that, but he also planted a lot of ground provisions. We actually grew the yams on that estate I remembered that, and he worked hard. I mean he was out of the house before seven every morning and he didn't come back in until six, and my mother worked hard too; she was working at the land to as well as looking after the household.

Alex Bruno: What would have been her name and where was she from?

Dame Eugenia: Josephine Charles, she was born in Point Mitchel too. She was one of six sisters and I remember like when- the story we have in the family is that my father was "courting" her and my grandmother, my mother's mother asked him when was he going to get serious about it and he said "When my lime trees blossom, not before." But he had land on the coast going up to Soufriere, Derochelle, very difficult land. We didn't have any land where you could drive a car to it you always had to walk almost on our fours to get to it you know but he worked hard and he saved and he knew what was important and what wasn't important, and he used his money carefully, and that way he was able to look after his family and to make sure that his family was better off than he had been; to get more education than he had had and had a chance to become professional people, and, so I have a great admiration from my grandparents and my parents, because without them we wouldn't have nothing at all. We wouldn't have had the mind, the ambition to know that we could go further than we were, and so I admire them for that.

Alex Bruno: Your family - how many members I mean constitute your immediate family?

Dame Eugenia: Two brothers and myself; there were two girls and two boys.

The sister she became a nun and she died in Europe, she was a nun in France, and there were two boys. Both boys became doctors - that was their choice to become doctors.

Alex Bruno: What is the status of them now?

Dame Eugenia: Oh, they are retired now. One of them is retired in Antigua he retired twice. He retired in the Caribbean and afterwards working in Jamaica he retired there. He lives in Antigua, and he is married to an Antiguan they live there, and I have a brother in Barbados who married a Barbadian and lives in Barbados and he was a doctor too, he worked in Barbados and Trinidad.

Alex Bruno: Can you call the names of your brothers?

Dame Eugenia: Yes, my brothers – the one in

Barbados is Rene Charles, and the one in Antigua is Lawrence Charles.

Alex Bruno: And your sister who had passed on?

Dame Eugenia: Jane Charles, and she died as a nun in France.

Alex Bruno: Where did you come in on the family tree?

Dame Eugenia: The last child.

Alex Bruno: You were the last child. How did that make you feel, you being the last? Girl?

Dame Eugenia: Well, fine, I mean… I think I had more time with my; it seems to me I had more time living with my parents but that isn't so. I mean my brothers lived with them until he went away to study, but I, I found that I had good companionship for my parents.

I had a great respect for them.

Alex Bruno: Dame Eugenia, it appears to me as I'm speaking with you now, that you were not always rich, I was, it is… it is…

Dame Eugenia: Never had! We had never been rich. My father owned a small piece of land which was at the top of a mountain.

Dame Eugenia: You will never get a road to that place you had to walk up to it, and they planted coffee and they planted yams and they planted limes after a time. They had to have horses; he - had to go down every morning early to bathe the horse in the sea at Point Mitchel and come back up, and then walk back down to school, and he did that all his, all his young life.

Alex Bruno: So, why is it most times especially,

and we will get to that in a little while when doing your family now your political career; why is it that it has been said, politically, that you do not know the plight of people who have gwayé so to speak to grow up?

Dame Eugenia: Because they just think, because, and I think it is a compliment to my father, he knew how to use his money he knew where to use his money and he was really cautious and careful with his money, and we learnt that like you don't spend money you haven't got. You don't borrow money. You must work for it and use it after you borrowed it…after you've, you've earned it!

Alex Bruno: Okay, you the girl —

Dame Eugenia: My father never borrowed money to send his children to school, he earned and make sure it was there in the bank before he required it.

Alex Bruno: So, your father was truthfully a rich man?

Dame Eugenia: He was not, he was never rich! He worked hard and he lived on the money he made, but he made his plans well ahead of time so that he could make the money to see his plans come into fruition.

Alex Bruno: You said he made most of his money by doing his agricultural practices?

Dame Eugenia: Always. That's what he did, he was an agriculturist. He was a peasant; he was a small peasant.

Alex Bruno: Later on, he introduced a major institution in Dominica some sort of -

Dame Eugenia: The Co-operative Bank, because he wasn't owing himself. Mr. P. I Boyd was very influential in that. The idea was, people – you see, we didn't have any credit unions in those days when they opened the credit union in Roseau. He said, if credit unions had been there before I probably would have never designed the Co-operative Bank, because the idea was people with little income could save their money and make that money do things for them. So, then they use to call it the penny bank because you could actually go and put a penny in your savings account. You didn't have to have a lot of money to save. Any little bit of money you had you could put it there, and then you could use it or you could use the money you had in the bank, that's collateral for you to borrow money to do things better for yourself. There are a lot of people who began life with ice cream churners on the street. They borrowed the money because they had saved pennies in the Co-operative Bank, they could borrow money to buy a new ice cream tub, and from that they made money and kept saving money until they could own a house. Well, most of Goodwill was built up by money from the Co-operative Bank and that was small peoples' money.

Alex Bruno: How old would you have been then when this bank was established?

Dame Eugenia: Oh, I don't remember nah…I was… it was established before I went away to study, I know that so I must have been about 16 - 15, 16 and then I came back and then I came back and found it going and I worked- I was the secretary at the Bank after a while and then I was Director of the Bank and late then - for instance at one time they wanted to increase my father's salary because things were doing better and he refused it. He said no, we must leave all the money we can there for the little person to be able to borrow to make life better for himself.

Alex Bruno: What position did he give himself at the Bank?

Dame Eugenia: He was Managing Director of the Bank. Nobody got loan there unless he saw the person and talk with the person, and he would advise the people. For instance, people would come to borrow money to build a house and he would sit down and tell them why you building such a big house you only have two children? He would take interest in the matter as if it was his own and he would go on the spot and see that the work was being done properly for the person, so people were well secured when they borrowed from the Co-operative Bank. I tell you, most of the people at Goodwill who have houses there got it as a result of a loan from the Co-operative Bank.

Alex Bruno: Dame Eugenia you seem to be making a lot of emphasis on family. You really, emm to me, appear to me you really strong family person?

Dame Eugenia: I think that's where, that's where, your life begins. If you have a good strong family, understanding if you can get on well with your family you can get on well the community. Well, that's where you begin to live with people in your family and you have to respect each person in the family as having their own mind their own ideas, and you having your own mind own ideas but working together to make things work, and that's the beginning of community life.

Alex Bruno: So, no doubt this feature we doing on you which we have to call the name that is being called One Hundred Great Dominicans - you as one of the persons that has been nominated by an overwhelming majority of people - will would have to include a lot of the flavor, of the family flavor?

Dame Eugenia: Family life is the most important thing. If you have a good family life you have a successful family life, and if you understand how to work with a family in a family, then you will also understand how to work in a community, and you can't build a country unless you have good community living you know.

Alex Bruno: Well, let's tell me a little more about you. We now seem to have a very clear idea as to how you were - your composition of your family composition – the composition of your family.

Tell us a little about you, like when you were –

Dame Eugenia: We never consider, we never even thought of ourselves as having money none of the children thought we were rich. I mean your books, you had to get books at school and they never stinted you. They found the money for you to own your own books so you could continue your studies. You had clothes - very strict on that I had three new dresses a year and no more and I had to make that do; I didn't even stop to think you could have four; more to me… three new dresses a year because I was growing fast, all of us became very tall and I would have one cotton dress to wear in the afternoons, and one for Corpus Christi and one for Christmas and that was the end of it and those clothes had to last you for the whole two years.

The same thing with shoes, you know.

Alex Bruno: So, you grew up very strict, no wonder you acquired the name -

Dame Eugenia: And you had no…you were not allowed to think that money was an important thing. It was hard work that was the important thing, it was respect to other people that was the important thing and, you know, we always had a maid helping us in the house but she was like part of the family. She lived with us like part of the family. I mean I could not be rude to our maid I would get a good swiping on my backside.

Alex Bruno: Hence the acquisition of the name, *"The Iron Lady,"* later on in your life?

Dame Eugenia: I don't think so. I just think people have to learn to do things properly and you have to have reasons for doing things. you don't go flying around like a bat in the dark.

Alex Bruno: You were - what year were you born?

Dame Eugenia: 1919.

Alex Bruno: And that would have been in Point Mitchel?

Dame Eugenia: Yeah, I was born in point Michel; we came down to live in Roseau when I was two years old.

Alex Bruno: Where in Roseau?

Dame Eugenia: In Old Street. Where am… opposite Gabriel's place.

Alex Bruno: Okay

Dame Eugenia: I remember when we moved from Point Mitchel to make our home here, the house was there before and my father put an attic on it so we each- so I always had a bedroom of my own which is a luxury I think among people, but that's because he build an attic so each of us had a room.

Alex Bruno: Two years you moved from Point Mitchel and you remembered vividly?

Dame Eugenia: I remembered that because my sister was older than me, was already living in Roseau with relatives… of my father and she came to make her home with us when we came to Roseau.

Alex Bruno: What schools did you attend?

Dame Eugenia: I went to the, Miss Rock use to have a little infant school in Roseau and I went to that I must have been three years old when they send me to school, my mother sent me there to get me out the house

I think and send me school. And then I went to the Convent when I was six.

Alex Bruno: Miss Rock, what was Miss Rock's first name?

Dame Eugenia: I don't remember now, we always called her Miss Rock, she lived at Marlborough Street.

Alex Bruno: And Convent at six and then you went to the Convent High School of course?

Dame Eugenia: I went to the - I went to the Convent High School like when I did my senior there, I went to Grenada to school to do my matriculation. Because they were not teaching Latin here at the girls' school and I had to do Latin. Decided I was going to do law already, so I had to do Latin. I had to have Latin before I was admitted to do Law so I went to Grenada for a year, did the matriculation in Grenada with the Latin and then I went straight to Canada cause in that time there was the War on and the University of Toronto had arranged for us to come and do work to study there, because they weren't keen on having all the students in London when there was so much bombing going on.

Alex Bruno: So, at what age did you attend High school here in Dominica?

Dame Eugenia: I must have gone there at six and I must have left there when I was fourteen or fifteen… I had finished my senior exams.

Alex Bruno: Oh, so you did, it was an entire cause of study from six?

Dame Eugenia: Yes, I went right through into senior Cambridge and then from there I went to Grenada to do my matriculation, because I wanted to do Latin and they taught it in

	Grenada, they didn't teach it here.
Alex Bruno:	To girls?
Dame Eugenia:	I went to boarding school in Grenada.
Alex Bruno:	You can't remember the name of the school?
Dame Eugenia:	Yes, the Convent high School in Grenada. It was a Convent School too in St. Georges.
Alex Bruno:	What's the history behind the convent school do you know, can you tell us?
Dame Eugenia:	No, it's just there for a long time. The Shillingfords went to school there too. A. C Shillingford's daughters went to school there before me in Grenada and so I went as a border there to learn, to do my matriculation exams so I do Latin

and there was a good teacher there at the Convent there…so I could enroll into Law afterwards.

Alex Bruno: Who were the school mates of yours at school that you remembered now around here in Dominica still?

Dame Eugenia: Mrs. Agatha Shillingford, she is sister to the um past president and she now lives, I went to see her last week, she lives up at Morne Prosper, and um Helen Trotter. She died since, but she has children you know the Trotter family, and these were the people I was closest to.

Alex Bruno: So, you said you move out to Canada after your matriculation exams in Grenada?

Dame Eugenia: I went to do Law in Toronto. They made a special arrangement for those of us in the Caribbean who want to do Law, not to come to London where there was so much bombing going on with the War, so we could - if we did the degree at Toronto- we could be admitted that would take at the first part the bar exam then we could go to London and do the second half of the bar exam.

Alex Bruno: Where in Toronto, what school?

Dame Eugenia: University of Toronto.

Alex Bruno: And that would have been in what year 19...?

Dame Eugenia: I went there from 1940 to 1946. I entered there 1940 and I left, I graduated in 1946.

Alex Bruno: Tell me a little about the Second World War. What you know about it or what you know now?

Dame Eugenia: I was in Toronto most of the time. We were following it very keenly of course, we were interested -

every day we want to know the news, what happened how we getting on; were the Allies winning or what. So, we were very keen following the news at the time, all of us in Canada, but it was an important thing to us. And all of us were there because there was a war on first of all.

Alex Bruno: Give us a little history about the War. For those of us who were not around how did the war get started, what about the war tell me?

Dame Eugenia: Well, when… it'd nothing to do with us. We always starting wars in Dominica now with our own people, but it was nothing to do with us, it was the fact that there…it was, it was in Europe when one European country wanted to dominate another European country and so this, this come up and they went to war about it.

And the British were anti-German, the Germans were anti-British and they fought strongly and then they got the Americans to join them to fight in Europe for the freedom of Europe really, to make sure that each country in Europe could continue on its own without domination by another country.

Alex Bruno: The Germans of course being assisted by the US?

Dame Eugenia: No, no, no the US fought with the Germans.

Alex Bruno: They fought with?

Dame Eugenia: They fought against the Germans, yes. The Germans were on their own. They had taken some countries around them, but it wasn't that those countries were willing to be part of them so they were; they had internal strife all the time.

Alex Bruno: To the best of your knowledge, and I know you would know, how did this war escalate to become a world war?

Dame Eugenia: Well, the Germans attacked some of the European countries and so the British and the Americans fought with these countries that were attacked by the Germans to put the Germans off, and so it escalated and of course because Britain had all these countries that were part of the empire, like the Australians and the South Africans they all came and help the British to fight and we to in the Caribbean sent people to fight too.

Alex Bruno: So, we supported the Allied party?

Dame Eugenia: Yes, we were part of the Allies.

Alex Bruno: How did that War help to influence and frame your life as a boarding professional?

Dame Eugenia: It didn't have a lot of effect on me except it changed the way I studied. I would not have gone to Canada to study if we haven't had the war; it's because of the war that the British had decided that we do some of our things outside of London, because London was being bombed badly all the time, they didn't want so many young students around the place. So, in that way it affected me that I didn't move at (Inaudible) …in Canada, and I was really pleased that I did stay in Canada in a really different way. If I had gone to Britain straight, I would not have had the same experience that I had by going to Canada to study.

Alex Bruno: But you did your final exams in London, Britain?

Dame Eugenia: Oh yes, I had to do it- my bar in Britain. So, I went back and studied for a year in Britain and did my bar.

Alex Bruno: How did you do? Tell me.

Dame Eugenia: I did alright. I worked hard and I got through.

Alex Bruno: I like the way you say that. So, what do you hold right now in terms of a Law degree?

Dame Eugenia: Well, I have a degree from Canada; a Bachelor of Arts in Law in Canada, in Honors Law, then I have the Barrister Law from London.

Alex Bruno: So, when you were finished you had to come back to Dominica, did you do something?

Dame Eugenia: I wasn't bound to come back, because I could have gone to Africa to work. I got an offer to go to Africa to work then, especially since, whilst I was in London, I had done some work on juvenile delinquencies and they were looking for magistrates for that, and so I was offered a job in the, the African countries to work as a magistrate for juveniles. But at that time my parents came up to London to visit me and I realized that I should go back home. They required some of us back home, because none of the children was home so I came back home to live with them and I enjoyed; I was glad I did. it was a good decision.

Alex Bruno: And that would have been what year and what was going on in Dominica at that time?

Dame Eugenia: In 1947. It work, and my father, at that time, was a member of the house...member of the House; it wasn't called Parliament then, it was called Legislative Council, and he was a member of that. He was strong; if you think I am strongly spoken, you are wrong, he was very strong! But in the end, I think that the British realized that he was a person who was interested in the country and they learn to respect him. But he was…he didn't hold his tongue; he told them exactly what he thought all the time.

Alex Bruno: From what age, from what year did he really get into Legislative Government?

Dame Eugenia: I can't remember what year he got in, but when I came in, he was there, he was in there. He the first Minister of Education in Dominica you know. When the ministerial system came, he was the first Minister of Education and Social Services –

Alex Bruno: So, he –

Dame Eugenia: Health, Education and Social Services.

Alex Bruno: So, he served for -

Dame Eugenia: Yes, and the… he, he, when we got universal suffrage, when everybody got to vote here, he ran and that's when he became the minister. It was thought that he wouldn't win because he was not, tipep (not easy) you know, but he, but people recognize his sincerity and the ambition he had for Dominicans you know.

Alex Bruno: Did he influence you some how to make a decision?

Dame Eugenia: No, no. He was against my going into politics. Both my mother and father were against it; they said why don't you just stay and do your work and forget about people. You know they used to tell me, people will want to fight with you because of the statement you making, I said Well somebody has to make statements so. But they were not pleased that I had gone into politics, but I, I couldn't resist it. There were things that required doing and they were not being done, and so I couldn't see it without opening my mouth and saying what I thought, you know.

Alex Bruno: So, you allowed him to have his say in forty-seven [1947]. For how long after, and what you did in the interim before you decided to get into politics?

Dame Eugenia: Oh, I was, I was working in my Law office; I was working hard because I had to support myself, my father wasn't supporting me; I had to earn a living. So, I was working in my Law office and making money, and making money on very small amounts. A person came to you to write a letter for them and two dollars- and you wrote the letter, you know, you didn't get big fees in those days because nobody had money to pay big fees, but I enjoyed the work.

I enjoyed working as a lawyer. I enjoyed all the years that I spent working for people, and people coming to you with their problems, you can explain to them what they doing wrong, how they should go and I enjoyed that.

Alex Bruno: Do you remember your first client you might have served?

Dame Eugenia: The first client I had was a man, he'd been- a woman had brought him up for an affiliation order; for a child born out of wedlock and the man came to me to defend him and I was very proud of that, he had come to a woman layer to defend him (chuckle) and not a man lawyer.

Alex Bruno: What happened? What transpired?

Dame Eugenia: I won the case (chuckles).

Alex Bruno: So, you won your first case?

Dame Eugenia: That's right.

Alex Bruno: So, you worked for how many years before you got into public life in terms of gov… I mean um politics, so to speak?

Dame Eugenia: I think it was in forty-eight we began to look at what was happening and decided that we required a new party so, we formed a new party; it wasn't…I didn't inherit a party, we had to form a party and begin from the beginning; from scratch with it. So, we formed, and we called it the Freedom Party. Because what had happened is that I used to write articles in the paper, criticizing things that government was doing, and the government were mad and they decided they would stop it. So, they wanted people to tell them who had written the articles, I wasn't ashamed of it, perhaps I didn't sign them I don't remember really, but they wanted to stop me writing articles and I wasn't going to stop because there were things to be corrected and I wanted them corrected. So that's how I began, and they decided to pass a law which we, which we called *The Shut Your Mouth Bill* because they didn't- they wanted to prevent you writing articles in the press. Well, the press didn't agree with them and I didn't agree with them so the articles continued, but they tried to pass a law called *The Shut Your Mouth Bill* and we had…and they declared that no public meeting should be held in Roseau, but they forgot that Goodwill was not part of Roseau, so we had the meetings in Goodwill at the Lindo Park. And at that meeting we told the people you know they going to pass a Law, it said you must not have freedom of speech, and I think you should come to the House to hear them pass that Law against you, so, there was a demonstration. People marched up that morning to the House and those who could get in got in but here was enough room for everybody to get in, and so they spend and the people were there and honestly, they were applauding me and they, they passed the bill; they still passed the bill but there was an uproar as a result and in fact whilst we were demonstrating there, they sent to call me to come and talk to them. That must have been, I don't know I don't think… I'm thinking that I went to the government headquarters but it wasn't built yet I don't think; any way they sent to call me, so I went down to talk to them I said if you pass that bill you will have trouble in Dominica you got to let it go, they are telling you they don't want it! They want the right to talk. So, I became enemy number one of any government that ever came into government.

Alex Bruno: That would have been what year?

Dame Eugenia: That was sixty-eight, I think.

Alex Bruno: Oh. In sixty-eight you decided to form the party?

Dame Eugenia: That's when we had the demonstration and then we went out to the country telling people that we must have the right to say what happened to us in our country so it was as a result of that we formed the Freedom Party.

Alex Bruno: So, from forty-eight to sixty-eight you were involved in mobilizing the -

Dame Eugenia: Not really. I was working in my office I wasn't… I knew what was happening, I was expressing myself but I wasn't in politics no.

Alex Bruno: So, when you said them and they were trying to pass

'The Shut Your Mouth Bill' who would have been the "they"?

Dame Eugenia: The Labour Party, Patrick's party - no it was under Leblanc and when we had the demonstration, we asked permission to march so we had a march from Pottersville all the way up to at that time, the ministry building, was at the back of the court the High Court you know, where the Public Works is, so we went there and when we spoke. Leblanc came out in the gallery and said um… I am here to rule and rule.

Inaudible…

Alex Bruno: …Associated Statehood?

Dame Eugenia: Yes, we were not independent yet. You hear the story that I was against independence **(Inaudible)**, I spoke to the people on the radio about independence.

I have offered to send them the tape of what I was going to say if they thought something was bad, they could take it out I wasn't… They were the government they had a right to control, but they refuse to let me speak on the radio. But when they were talking independence in England, the British insisted that there should be members of the Opposition on the team and myself, Lennox Honychurch and Mr. Moise went…to represent the Opposition, and I said the statement that I thought the citizens of Dominica should know what independence means and they should be told from all sides what it means. and the government refuses to let me talk on the radio, and the government told them that they would not get an independence date until they had allowed the citizens to be informed by all sides you know.

So, we went round we had thirty (30) meetings around the country talking to people, but plain out meetings on the road sides you know, in the school, hall and something… and let people ask questions and tell them what it meant and what they would have to do and their duties as citizens, and after that the British agreed to give us Independence.

Alex Bruno: So, you never really –

Dame Eugenia: I never opposed it, but I wanted the citizens to know what it was because they were being told independence- they will be able to do what they want, that is not true. With independence, you become responsible for yourself so that you to be careful how you spend your money, whether you have money to spend, and you must choose the right ways to do it and this is what I wanted the citizens to understand, because once they became independent it was their job to make things work. It wasn't only the government. it was also the citizens job to make it work.

Alex Bruno: Dame Eugenia I was told you wanted independence to be under your reign that's why you —

Dame Eugenia: No, I wasn't…I didn't know I was going to win the election there were only three of us in the house at the time, Moise, Lennox Honychurch and myself so it wasn't um….

Alex Bruno: Okay, now the party was formed —

Dame Eugenia: I wanted the citizens of Dominica to understand what independence meant because they were be given the idea that when they are independent, life will be a glory. T's isn't true, you are responsible all your own, responsible for all your expenditure to you have to make the money to run the country through independence. Nobody owes you a living after that.

Alex Bruno: And you were satisfied that they knew then at the time we got independence?

Dame Eugenia: Yes, because I was given the chance then to talk to them. We went round… they refused to let me talk on the radio to them. I complained to the British about it but we went round the country and held about thirty-three meetings all-round the country, sit down in school class rooms so people could ask questions, you could tell them what you think and what you want, and it was we, our party that decided that we should become a republic right away.

Alex Bruno: Who we, who we?

Dame Eugenia: The Freedom Party. We decided and when we went to Britain. We went with that and we wanted it to go republic right away and the reason was this, that we were… our government was very much in co with the Guyanese government, they took all the instructions from Barnham, and we knew that if we went independent not as they think a month after wards they would want to go into a republic and I didn't; and we would not have had the British helping us to formulate the constitution and we didn't know anything about constitutions I mean we had never been a country before. I didn't want Guyana to give us what they had because I wasn't satisfied if Guyana had the right thing, so I wanted to go straight into republic so we would have advice of Constitutional Law in England to

	help us put a good government in place.
Alex Bruno:	A number of Caribbean countries had gone ahead with independence before us why did you think it was going to be a trouble?
Dame Eugenia:	Well, Trinidad and Jamaica and Barbados were ahead of us in many ways: Economical they were ahead of us and even in the constitutions they were ahead of us too, so that is why they were able to go earlier into it.
Alex Bruno:	Your party was formed in 1968 you said?
Dame Eugenia:	I think so.
Alex Bruno:	There was a DUPP before, wasn't that your party also?
Dame Eugenia:	No, no. There was an opposition

	party before we were formed, but I wasn't in politics before. I was never in a party before that.
Alex Bruno:	So, the DUPP wasn't formed by you or —
Dame Eugenia:	No, no, no, no.
Alex Bruno:	Who?
Dame Eugenia:	Baron was in, was head, Franklin Baron was head of DUPP but I wasn't in that, I never belonged to that.
Alex Bruno:	So, what —
Dame Eugenia:	I criticized quite often, when I was at it, I criticized when the DUPP had done things.
Alex Bruno:	So, the story is that DUPP was an extension of the Freedom Party and Freedom Party is an extension of DUPP?

Dame Eugenia: Well of course Leblanc thought so, Leblanc thought that he looked after the poor and we looked after the rich and I didn't think that there was a rich or poor- we looked after the country and there were no really very rich people in Dominica at that time.

Alex Bruno: So, your party was never a bourgeois party so to speak?

Dame Eugenia: Of course not! Well, a lot of us were lawyers if you make that bourgeois but I mean we just happened to have been lawyers and it was because we were lawyers, we were looking at what was happening and seeing, analyzing what was happening illegally. But we were not a, we were never a bourgeois party.

Alex Bruno: You didn't look for a particular with a class of people?

Dame Eugenia: Of course not! I mean they all

thought my father was a rich man really because they didn't see people selling my father's property. He made sure he paid his debts that is, that was in which he would deprive himself of other things to make sure he didn't owe and I learnt that from him; that you are not in comfortable position when you owe.

Alex Bruno: So who are the people who helped you the original people?

Dame Eugenia: One people who gave us a lot of help was Mr. Roberts, Loftus Roberts, He had been a civil servant and I suppose what is now a PS (Permanent Secretary). I don't think there were PS in those days. And we worked a lot with him you know. He was a very sound, solid person and he would help keep us on the straight and narrow path, and people like that we worked with.

Alex Bruno: So, who were the Pioneering members of the Dominica Freedom Party?

Dame Eugenia: Well, I was and Mr. Alvin Arma Trading who died the other day he was very important to us and who had a good relationship with the French and that is how I think our relationship with the French became so strong. And we had um… Mr. Maynard and Mr. Alleyne. Mr. Baron who had been in the previous party who had been in the party before us and who I disagreed with a lot when he was in the government, but he worked with us after we formed the party. Mr. Alleyne, Brian Alleyne's father was um… became one of us afterwards so…
I think he begun on his own before we formed our party but he came in with us.

Alex Bruno: Elkin Henry?

Dame Eugenia: Yes, Elkin Henry was a member of our party but then he wanted to- he was undisciplined and we… and up to now he's been like that. He didn't like that the council of the party has to choose the person to run for us in election and Elkin was not chosen to run, and he decided he was going to run. So, he ran against our member and so we dismissed him from the party. Either you are with the Party or against it but when he um, he thought he had won the election - I don't know in the count and he called Leblanc and told him I am your man, and we got to know that so when they had the final count, he lost, so we left him with Leblanc. (chuckles)

Alex Bruno: He lost by just about –

Dame Eugenia: By one vote, yes.

Alex Bruno: I don't think he took that very

lightly he still thinks that am it might have been manipulated?

Dame Eugenia: But but it wasn't Freedom Party who had counting the votes you know it was the Labour Party cause they were the party in power it wasn't us counting the votes. (chuckles)

Alex Bruno: So he was left high and dry?

Dame Eugenia: Yeah.

Alex Bruno: You do not go against Dame Eugenia Charles and succeed; is that a true statement?

Dame Eugenia: No. No I think that you had no right to belong to a party and at the same time to foster another party. You cannot belong to a party, run for the party and when you win, ring the leader of the other party and tell them I'm your man? if you're their man go with him and don't stay with us!

You must be honest in everything you do. I mean you must be open, not deceive in what you are doing you know.

Alex Bruno: So, Dame Eugenia your party was formed and your life had change, had been changed. You still a lawyer a practicing lawyer but you had aspirations to run; to be in government?

Dame Eugenia: Not really. I didn't think of that I was just, wanted Dominica to be a better place for Dominicans to live in.

Alex Bruno: So how were you going to get that done?

Dame Eugenia: Well, doing…by making sure the citizens knew what they wanted and now pronounced it. People, must know, have respect for the citizens' voice. I still think strongly that the citizens are the ones who run the country but they must make up their mind about things, they must inquire about things and they must make decisions about things, and more forward with those decisions.

Alex Bruno: So at what stage in your life did you decide to take this thing seriously and aspire?

Dame Eugenia: When I, when we formed the party and we had some of us in the House we worked as a party to make sure that we got the things we expressed the views of people to get the things we wanted for the country. And so on and so we were exercising our rights as citizens who saw where Dominica should go.

Alex Bruno: Leblanc was a very smart man was he, or is he?

Dame Eugenia: Well, he disliked me. He thought that I was a bourgeois I was no more bourgeois than Mr. Leblanc.

	Leblanc had owned much more land than I did.
Alex Bruno:	At what stage in your life did you become a millionaire?
Dame Eugenia:	I've never become a millionaire; I'm still not a millionaire. I'm living on a pension I think that's always a thousand and forty-nine dollars ($1,049.00) a month. That's what the government pays after twenty-five (25) years in parliament and that's what am living on.
Alex Bruno:	Dame Eugenia is not a millionaire?
Dame Eugenia:	No, I never have been. I've never thought of myself as being a person who had who had everything I wanted, I've never had everything I wanted.
Alex Bruno:	When Leblanc decided to step down and hand over to Patrick in

the seventy's (70s) in the late sixties, seventies?

Dame Eugenia: I think he was at first thinking of handing over to Armour you remember that? It was a confusion about this I don't know but there was confusion about then in the - and Patrick got the vote I think with the party to lead the country. I think it was a bad thing for the Dominica because Patrick didn't have a thought in his head but looking after himself.

Alex Bruno: And you-

Dame Eugenia: That was a bad page in our history Patrick becoming the person in change.

Alex Bruno: And you thought, then, that you going to do all you could to destabilize him?

Dame Eugenia: No, but I thought we must more and more teach the people what to look for because I have said, I think a country is run by citizens and the citizens must be knowledgeable and must understand what's it all about and must make choices.

Alex Bruno: So, Patrick became Premiere and then he was heading towards independence and you became after being in the opposition for almost twenty years then, you became -

Dame Eugenia: No I wasn't in opposition all that time because I didn't go into the House until about sixty-eight (1968) you know.

Alex Bruno: It would have been like?

Dame Eugenia: Four or five years.

Alex Bruno: Oh so you were not in the house until sixty-eight (1968)?

Dame Eugenia: No.

Alex Bruno: But your party was formed in Okay -

Dame Eugenia: About the same year they had an election.

Alex Bruno: So, all the story about your party being an extension of DUPP?

Dame Eugenia: No, no that never happened we never had no deal with DUPP.

Alex Bruno: You got in the house in sixty-eight (68) and then about seventy-four (1974) seventy-five (1975) you started mounting your pressure to get -

Dame Eugenia: We were working all the time pressuring, insisting that Dominicans make up their own mind on what they want. They must not just listen to people. They must think for themselves and make choices for themselves.

Alex Bruno: So, you got an opening because of

a weak link you thought in Patrick?

Dame Eugenia: No, no, no what happened was Patrick allowed… there was oh yes, they were going to pass a law in the House what is it again they were going to pass? And the people demonstrated they surrounded the House. I can't remember nuh… the same "Shut up your mouth Bill".

Alex Bruno: The same one that, the original one about Leblanc?

Dame Eugenia: Yes, and they were going to pass the 'Shut Your Mouth Bill' and the people were, talked for a long time against it… you see the trade unions, the editors of newspapers were against it because it was against them, so they couldn't express their view so they had meetings at the Parish Hall to talk about it. I didn't go to any of these meetings I was busy going out to talk to people on the ground, like the night before they had the plan to stop the House I wasn't there. I had gone to Soufriere to talk to people tell them what was happening and then it was that day they were going to pass the law the people demonstrated. They surrounded the House of Assembly down you know at the government headquarters and they were… I actually heard Patrick on the telephone calling out to the army - for the army to come. and move those people and we had no right to talk and we decided what we going to do and so am… and I overheard him saying that on the phone. He was talking from the Registrar's office which was the high court and the House of Assembly which was the same in those days. So I went, the soldiers came down and began firing shots and some people got killed and that caused a lot of disturbance. A lot of people who had been pro-Patrick were anti him for that, for allowing that to happen.

Alex Bruno: I was told that events have been influenced by you, orchestrated by Charles Savarin?

Dame Eugenia: Well, unions were strongly against what was happening, the unions and the newspapers, the editors of newspapers they thought it was against freedom of speech, but it wasn't anything to do with that. They - it was the citizens of Dominica who decided to come out and tell Patrick they don't want what he is going to do. But he was determined to go through with it. He was a stubborn man and he didn't listen to what anybody told him, so, I don't think he got advice from his fellow cabinet members any way. I think he did he what he wanted to do. They had no say in what he was doing.

Alex Bruno: Mamo, do you not like Patrick?

Dame Eugenia: Well, I dislike a man who is prepared to betray his country. I thought it was a terrible thing for him to do, for him to plot with Ku Klux Klan people; people who hate Negros to come over and take the country. The Ku Klux Klan were going to come and take Dominica but they were going to make it a drug place; they were going to make drugs here and manufacture drugs and ship them abroad, I mean I couldn't let that happen, I couldn't live in a country that was doing that, I would have to leave.

Alex Bruno: How did you know that?

Dame Eugenia: Because I got the information from people who were in part of it.

Alex Bruno: Patrick says there is no evidence of that and he totally denied it?

Dame Eugenia: The people went to jail in America for plotting with him. Canada and America. I gave evidence in a case in Canada on that. They had letters and so on they had exchanged, because of the plot to take, you know to take over the country.

Alex Bruno: Dominica?

Dame Eugenia: Yes, it was with the people like Ku Klux Klan and people who believe in that sort of thing you know, People who don't like black people. Why would you want to tell the Ku Klux Klan about Dominica nuh? You know what I mean? You know it was bad.

Alex Bruno: You just said he wouldn't have been able as a black man to influence a white supremacy group to come down because it –

Right, because they were going to take over the country! They weren't doing it for him. They were going to come over because they already plotted that they would have a manufacturing, a factory to make drugs where they could ship to Europe and make money on, all that was part of the plan. There were documents that put in court saying that, it wasn't I who made it up you know. The documents were put in court saying that.

Alex Bruno: So they were… Okay, so what role Patrick played in all the organization, the new party, the new country so to say? What would Patrick benefit from that - from selling the country?

Dame Eugenia: Well, they were going to make him… the idea was they were going to join Barbados and Dominica as one country and Patrick was to be president of the joint country and that's what he wanted, to be a big shot! I don't know how he a big shot and he don't have any money in your hand to do things for the people that really count, the people who support him.

Alex Bruno: So, you organized a protest to put him off?

Dame Eugenia: I didn't organize protest; there was a meeting the night before, I wasn't at meeting. I had gone to Soufriere to talk to the people to tell them what was happening in town, and at that meeting, it was decided that they should not allow the Bill to pass, they should surround the House and prevent the meeting being held.

Alex Bruno: Charles Savarin was the main person, they called him the agitator?

Dame Eugenia: No, he was head of a union and all the unions had got together on that basis.

Alex Bruno: So why is he the only person getting all the blows?

Dame Eugenia: Because he is the Freedom Party and so they must give the Freedom Party blows that's the only reason. But he was part - well of course the Civil Service Union was strong because there was a lot of educated people were in the civil service and they were strong, and of course if they went on strike government couldn't continue working cause they were strong in that when they pulled their Labour out, they left government almost I mean with no arms to work.

Alex Bruno: So it was a major co-incidence that um –

Dame Eugenia: All the unions got together and all

the journalists got together. The newspapers got together with them because it was against law, some of the law was against the journalists, against the newspapers not publishing what they wanted… in government giving them permission on they wanted to print you know.

Alex Bruno: What can you tell me about the lawlessness that took place during the protest in seventy-nine? um…

Dame Eugenia: The lawlessness was entirely to Patrick John's soldiers! They thought they had guns and they had shots and they must fire them, so some people got hurt and some people got killed.

Alex Bruno: Hurt by –

Dame Eugenia: I was in the parliament at the time and somebody called me, and I went out, and there was man, a dead man on the floor of the ministerial building, the ground floor. So I went back to parliament and I said you know if Dominicans feel so strongly about this law that they are prepared to fight and lose their life- one man has died, I just saw his body on the floor, I think we should just adjourn this to some other time. And (garbled)... said nothing doing! There was a little person, I can't remember now who he was, a member of parliament, he said "Nothing doing! We must pass the law; we must pass the law! We must pass the law!" So, they went ahead and pass the law. I think the law was still on the statute book but it's never been used.

Alex Bruno: I wanted to ask you, Patrick charged you and said that if the law was so bad why didn't you repeal it?

Dame Eugenia: I didn't have to bother repeal it because when it come up there would have been a dissension again when you were repealing it, because we were not the only people in the House so it stayed but it's never been used. Patrick doesn't dare use it today, why doesn't he use it today if it's so good? But the whole idea was that the people he had joined up with and… you know, what happened - is that we had arrested three (3) people, one (1) was the head of the army and I've forgotten who the two (2) others were now, and it was through what they said, while they were held at the police station, and we found out enough to be able to trace them… because, we, I called the Americans and said listen there is a person planning to come down here loading a gun, a boat with guns to come down here to attack us and the boat is being loaded in central airport.

Dame Eugenia: And the Americans sent their

people then and found the boat being loaded with the guns. It was part of news story in the thing.

Alex Bruno: There, there is a little thing I've been thinking of. If there was going to be an amalgamation between Barbados and Dominica and Patrick would have been the commander in chief or whatever wouldn't somebody in Barbados have had a say in terms…?

Dame Eugenia: No, the idea was that they were going to invade Barbados. They had arranged - there was a person from Barbados who was working in Europe and they had organized with, when they going to it, I've forgotten his name now. I don't think they could have succeeded quite frankly, because the Barbadians had an army, they were one of the few islands who had an army. But this is what the plan had been you know.

Alex Bruno: I was told the people who later became prominent members or who were then prominent members of your party were seen cutting posts and breaking people's homes and burning people's buildings and –

Dame Eugenia: I've never had any evidence of that, I've never been - nobody had ever complained to me about that and I think if it had happened somebody would have come and told me look at so and so of yours come and knock my house down, don't you think so? But nobody has ever made any complaint like that to me.

Alex Bruno: So that's news to you?

Dame Eugenia: It's news to me I've never heard this before.

Alex Bruno: So, you're totally clear in terms of organizing any form of lawlessness?

Dame Eugenia: The thing is that I went in the House of Assembly I complained about it when I knew that the man had been killed and shot, I asked that the house be adjourned because if the people, if the citizens of Dominica think so strongly here to take death rather than go through with it we must listen to them. But of course, Patrick said that's nonsense, he not bothering about that and we going ahead with our law. So they went ahead and passed it.

Alex Bruno: Who killed that young person who was killed? I believe his name was Phillip Timothy?

Dame Eugenia: No, Phillip Timothy wasn't the body I saw there, it was somebody else.

He was killed near his home because he was near his home watching the thing.

Alex Bruno: Oh, that other person but the big issue was around Phillip Timothy, surrounding his controversial?

Dame Eugenia: Because he wasn't part of the Freedom Party you know. His father use to be the gardener for Patrick John and he knew Patrick and he used to go there with his father. So, he knew Patrick John at the Morne, and it was he that - and he happen to be - because he came out to see what was happening and nobody killed him purposely; a shot passed, it killed him you know what I mean, they were firing shots and he got killed.

Alex Bruno: Is that the person's body you saw?

Dame Eugenia: No, no, no.

Alex Bruno: Phillip Timothy?

Dame Eugenia: No, no, no that was somebody else that was on the ground in front the House.

Alex Bruno: So, what is the issue, what can you say about Phillip Timothy? I was told about Defense Force and other people and who –

Dame Eugenia: Well, I think he was shot by the Defense Force because they were the ones who were shooting all over the place, but he was shot near his home he wasn't shot in the…I don't think he was shot… I don't think he was shot in government headquarters.

Alex Bruno: But the ballistics report I was told proved that he couldn't have been killed by the Defense Force bullet?

Dame Eugenia: But you know we had an enquiry on that. We got a judge from Jamaica to come and have an enquiry. If that was so wouldn't that evidence come out with the enquire? No such evidence came out to make us believe that it wasn't police, the army that shot him.

Alex Bruno: I was told that the document wasn't handy but in terms of wound it was not quite evident that it might have been?

Dame Eugenia: I don't know, I've never heard this before, just recently I've heard this story come out, but what am saying if there was evidence that the shot didn't come from an army… government why wasn't that make public at the time? you know what I mean.

Alex Bruno: Okay, so Dame we didn't even touch on, well we spoke of Independence and you spoke about the day… precede independence… you didn't actually speak about the day of independence. Were you a part of the independence ceremony?

Dame Eugenia: In fact the British insisted we should be on the team that spoke about independence in England, and so I went with Mr. Moise and Mr. Lennox Honychurch.

Alex Bruno: But on the event of –

Dame Eugenia: But then we came back and we spoke to Dominicans saying we are going to get independence, this is what you must make sure you get in your government, you know that sort of thing, educating the citizens on the idea of independence, so that the British insisted that I speak at the independence celebration, because they were coming down to give us independence and they wanted me to speak on the subject and I did.

Alex Bruno: So I was told you –

Dame Eugenia: I am very proud of my speech in fact.

Alex Bruno: Do you have your speech still?

Dame Eugenia: I'm sure I must have it somewhere.

Alex Bruno: I was told you wanted referendum instead?

Dame Eugenia: Well no, the British had said when they made us a state… an associated state we would get another referendum so I reminded them about it, but they knew the referendum would have gone against them and they wanted us off their hands so they didn't give the referendum. I didn't quarrel about it.

Dame Eugenia: I thought they should have kept their word and I said so, so once they didn't do it I went ahead - and understand that independence doesn't mean you going to have sweetness all over the place. You going to have to work for it you know.

Alex Bruno: But you would have been as proud as any other Dominican on that particular independence…night of independence?

Dame Eugenia: Yes! I knew we had taken on that burden and I didn't believe our government could handle that burden - the government we had at the time.

Alex Bruno: Okay for that time independence and just shortly after that, Patrick who very popular then - you would admit that he was popular during the independence?

Dame Eugenia: Yes, yes, oh yes. He was a popular man.

Alex Bruno: But following independence nine months after, all this happened, what we spoke about a while ago?

Dame Eugenia: Yes and therefore he was charged. No he was charged because, not charged for what happened, he was charged because of his plans with the people in America to come and take over the country; because another fella had… a Dominican in England had been part of it and had gone to Martinique and was arrested in Martinique and that sort of thing. So I knew that um, Patrick didn't mean good for Dominica you know, he just… and I think it was a mistake on the Labour Party's part to have make Patrick leader of their party. I think they did harm to Dominica doing that.

Alex Bruno: It was assumed he had done so many wonderful things before? I mean…

Dame Eugenia: He'd never done anything worthwhile. I have no respect for Patrick. I've never seen anything he did that I could admire.

Alex Bruno: He played for Dominica for 17 years in sports...

Dame Eugenia: Football? So that's something you'd make a prime minister of? You mean you really want a prime minister because he's good at football? I mean I don't agree with that.

Alex Bruno: He was one the youngest mayors of Roseau...

Dame Eugenia: Yes, but look at the scandals that went with him as the Mayor? Remember that? There were a lot of scandal around his mayorship you know.

Alex Bruno: He founded the Union, Waterfront and Allied.

Dame Eugenia: That's right. He didn't...the union was part of the Amalgamated Workers Union, and he took it out of there and made the workers, the WAWU separate from the

Amalgamated Workers Union.

Alex Bruno: And he seemed to have been a very influential young man, I mean…

Dame Eugenia: Perhaps he was, I don't know. He might… he might have had charisma but the fact is he was crooked! And he wanted power above everything else. He thought power was the most important thing in the world, and even if was the Ku Klux Khan would give it to him, he would take the Ku Klux Clan on board. And I couldn't see anybody who lived in Dominica wanting to have a relationship with the Ku Klux Khan. It just didn't make sense to me. And this stuff that came out in court you know, about his relationship with the Ku Klux Khan, and the correspondence that went on between them… wasn't anything I made up, it was something that he had written about…that he had sent people to Antigua to meet with people there to discuss this and put the plant together.

Alex Bruno: So his supporters, including him, who think that you might have undo or undone everything that he tried to do, is that the truth?

Dame Eugenia: He didn't do anything, there was nothing to undo because he didn't do anything.

Alex Bruno: The stadium?

Dame Eugenia: But he didn't do the stadium nah. He entered the agreement with the French for the French to do the stadium for us but he undertook that he would, that Dominica would plant the grass, Dominica would light the stadium and Dominica would make the um, what they call the places you sit on you know in the stadium… the stands. These are three most expensive parts of a stadium you know; lighting the stadium is the most expensive part you know of the stadium but he had undertaken to do that. Hurricane David came and knock down the walls that the French had put up, that's their part of the work, so soon as I got in I went to the French and I told then when are you going to finish the stadium? When are you going to take up work there again to finish the stadium for us? He told me not our stadium is your stadium. I said no you haven't given it to the government of Dominica yet, you have to finish it before you give it to us, and he say we not touching it again, we not going to do anything more to it, you must build the rest of it yourself. Well people were living in tents in the gardens, I could look after stadium and leave those people living in tents? What was more important, not to find for housing for those people? And that's what I did.

Alex Bruno: They put housing in the stadium –

Dame Eugenia: No, I put housing - I found money to do housing. First of all, the British give us the, (*inaudible*) …they give us Bath Estate so we could have housing there cause that didn't belong to us at the time you know, I was the one who got the British to give it to us.

Alex Bruno: And later on, you put factory sheds in the um-

Dame Eugenia: By that time now, the Americans were giving assistance to the countries in the Caribbean by putting factory sheds at their expense, and introducing investors to come and use those factory sheds so there would be work for people, and I thought it was more important to get work for people than to give them football to play in the afternoon.

Alex Bruno: You do not like sports at all…a lot?

Dame Eugenia: Yes, I do, but I do not think that people can have sports as more important than an empty stomach. I think we must have jobs to be able carry on the sports themselves.

Alex Bruno: Dame Eugenia you became Prime Minister of Dominica following the election of 1980, and that put you in a whole new light. Did you find, did it have a sense of vengeance in your heart when you got the office? No, I just realized it was a hard job because we didn't have any money to do things we were required to do, and we took the place after a hurricane. Almost every school had to be rebuilt or major repairs done to it. The only school that wasn't damaged in the hurricane was the school at Coulibistrie. Every other school was knocked flat and people was still living in the knocked out flat out schools because they had no other place to go to after the hurricane. So, I knew the country had to be rebuilt.

Alex Bruno: So you almost regretted I'm assuming the office of prime minister?

Dame Eugenia: No! I felt it was a challenge to do things for people and to get people themselves to do things, because people really reacted and work themselves to get the place in good order again. But it meant I had to go and beg for things from other countries. I…

End of Tape #1

An exclusive one-on-one Interview with Dame Eugenia Charles, conducted by Alex Bruno on Tuesday 30th December 1999, (11:05am – 1:20pm) at her office on Cork Street Roseau, Dominica.

Dame Eugenia
– Unedited

Tape #2

Continuing the interview with Dame Eugenia live here at the office in Cork Street Roseau…

Alex Bruno: Okay so Dame Eugenia we were saying that after the election, I mean after your first term in government you got an overwhelming, um, support from the people and you won even more con…

Dame Eugenia: Because we were doing things that they realize were required. We were trying to get them back into houses, we were trying to get the roads fixed. Well we had gone in there with intention of getting the roads fixed because our roads were in very poor condition and especially we wanted to get feeder roads so that farmers could get their crops from their field to the port. So this is what we are working on. We are looking for money for it. And I was fortunate and because I was a woman in a way, I got special consideration. So the man who was in charge in the European union, who was in charge of the Caribbean, was visiting Guadeloupe and the Guadeloupe government ask me to come to have lunch with him in Guadeloupe. They were sending a plane for me. I thought it was a good thing to do you know. So I went and of course because I was the most important woman there, I sat next to this man. So he told me he had just came from Grenada where they were asking him to help them to build their airport. We had been asking the Americans to build the airport in Grenada, but they'd ask him, so I said you mean you going to do airport for Grenada and you can't come and do roads for us in Dominica. You've done some roads here and gone over them with you heavy trucks and mash them up, you should come and put them back in order. He said you didn't ask me, so I said before you go back to France come and see it. So, he came and I drove him around the country and showed him what I wanted done. And he - the first repairs to the Portsmouth Road was done by them and he did the road to Castle Bruce because they had done it but they gone over it to do something else so they had mashed it up, so I made them do it again. He said you know what, I will arrange a meeting for you in Brussels and I will invite all the countries that I think can give you assistance. I will draft the letters and send them down to you for you to send to them, and you must come yourself and put your case accordingly so I thanked him. He did that. He drafted the letter, he decided who I should invite, he drafted the letters, sent it to me and I sent the letters out then I went. On the day I was - I arrived on a Sunday to hold the thing on the Monday, when I arrived there they told me you know he left Brussels yesterday. He has been made the Minister of Foreign

Affairs in France. They just had the election in mid-month in France, but he left everything in place. So we went to the meeting and we held the meeting and the World Bank undertook to do the arrangement for us. They (*inaudible*)...all the countries together with what they were going to give us, and they were going to get the experts to come and do the roads and teach us how to maintain roads. So, we - I got this, and it was only because the French, the French were very good to us you know. We would have had no health scheme, no health plans if it
hadn't been for the French. The French gave us a doctor in every village. They paid all the expenses; they gave the man a car, they didn't even ask us to give him a free license to drive the car they paid for that. It had nothing to do with us, and so as a result we had good health care in every village

which is a good thing. But the French - and the French was good to us. Everything, anything we wanted we could ask for it and they would give it to us.

Alex Bruno: Why? Why did the French love us so much?

Dame Eugenia: First of all, because we were next door and people used to go there for health care, so they thought if they could give us the health care we could keep our people here and look after ourselves which was a good thing. So, anyway, I got this road program so every road is fixed in Dominica within two years. By '82 all the roads were completed and it was all because the European Union had help me to get that assistance. I couldn't have got it by myself. I didn't know the people. They were the ones who knew the people to ask them for us.

Alex Bruno: You were very persuasive. Do you remember that man's name, you remember his name the person that you met who helped you with the roads?

Dame Eugenia: No, I don't remember his name now but he was the minister of foreign affairs and when I was going to India to a meeting of the um… 'travel'. I was going through France and he ask me to stay a day so he could meet me and have lunch with and talk with me and then I went on, so I was a day late for 'travel' in India.

Alex Bruno: It looks like the major activities around your life happen to have been, well starting in sixty eight (68), when you formed your party and even when you got into government. People sometime charge and say that you didn't do anything much, besides being a barrister or a lawyer?

Dame Eugenia: No, I was - I use to help to run the co-operative bank, which in there you learnt about people's need. People come and borrow money for the thing they had to do, you know what I mean? And then I helped build Fort Young. I was the main person they put at Fort Young. They had the old police station there which was moved, and I was able to get the CARICOM to help us to build Fort Young. So, a lot of things like that I did before I even was in government, and it was important that I was in government then.

Alex Bruno: So your second term came about and you started doing wonderful things for Dominica?

Dame Eugenia: First thing I wanted was the Bay front. I asked the British to give me – to fix the Roseau Bay Front. I said if you don't give it to us, the next storm we get will take

Roseau and you wouldn't give us back Roseau, so give us the Bay Front to prevent it. And they sent a team down, and I made the team come and talk to me before they sent in their report and I wasn't satisfied with what they were doing so I wrote. I called Margaret Thatcher and told her that the team you sent is no good get another team that understands us better. And she did send another team and that's how we got the Bay Front done. And when we got it, Edison James said it was a waste of money - the money should be given to the farmers instead you remember that? The other day he went to a meeting and he met the lady who was in charge, the minister who was in charge in England when we got the Bay Front, and he told her I've come to thank you for the Bay Front because we had three bad storms this year, and if we haven't had that, the town of Roseau would have gone. She said, "Oh you using the same words the last prime minister told me, and she told me if I didn't give her the Bay Front then I would lose Roseau and I wouldn't give her Roseau" and so I made sure that she got the Bay Front. And you could at least see that the money wasn't being wasted - it should be paid to farmers instead…if we had done that every farmer would have got six pence what would they have done with it? Bought a cigarette with it?

Alex Bruno: So you, I like the way you put it but maybe the farmers wouldn't like to heat that would they?

Dame Eugenia: They wouldn't have enough money to give them to do themselves better off- it was two million pounds. By the time it divide among the farmers everybody would have gotten a small amount of money which couldn't have help them to pay their debt. What the farmers really require is money to help them pay their debt so they - their land is free you know.

Alex Bruno: What if guys in office now seem to be putting some money to the farmers of late?

Dame Eugenia: But how much are farmers getting? They said they were giving them... um what they call it I've forgotten but, if you have to look at it the money Is not even enough for them to pay their debt. What the farmer wants is to make sure his land is off the bank's hands you know, so the bank can't come and take his land.

Alex Bruno: So, Dame I am one of those who had been very close to the Dominica Freedom Party and I personally believe that in the 1984 was the single, strongest year for the party.

I'm not too sure how you rate it but at that time of the party's history I believe the party was at its strongest.

Dame Eugenia: I don't know. I never stop to look to see whether people were strongest or not. I was looking at the things we had to do. And every day there was something new had - required being done in Dominica, and you really had to go and look for somebody to give you the money to do it because you didn't have the money yourself.

Alex Bruno: The men who worked with you, you being the first and woman Prime Minister of the Caribbean but the men who worked with you especially in cabinet were told or it was said, that they had no balls. They couldn't face up with you?

Dame Eugenia: Rubbish! Let me tell you what

was good about us and it's not being done now. Every Tuesday we had a cabinet meeting without fail from nine o'clock until we were finished and we, everybody had their say in that and it was not… sometimes I come with an idea and the others wouldn't approve it and my idea went, and their ideas went instead you know, because they were - I listened to them and I thought what they were doing, saying was right. I didn't always get what I wanted done because other people had ideas, but importantly… is that we were able… and every morning except Tuesday morning, not only did the ministers meet in cabinet but all the leaders in the different villages would come down.

Dame Eugenia: It was a Monday, I think on a Monday we use to have that except Tuesday, Monday. And you see they would come and tell you what was happening in the village. Sometimes they tell you the nurse has been away for the whole week and they haven't put somebody in her place so the minister would go and find out because a civil servant told him so - find out and make sure there is a nurse in place. So little things like that upsets people when they can't find service you know, so in that way we were close and we were close with the people in the village. We knew what was happening every week and we could do things for the people that were necessary.

Alex Bruno: So actually, the men who served with you could tell you when you were right and when you were wrong?

Dame Eugenia: Yes and they - it's not everything that I

wanted that I got and I come in there with an idea, and I'd listen to the others and their idea was better than and their idea would go through instead. I wasn't... it wasn't my opinion that went through.

Alex Bruno: Your party was charged of not attracting peasants; people of um humble um being - upbringing?

Dame Eugenia: Because they felt that we could give them more than they were getting. I don't blame the farmers they wanted more then they were getting and we could not give, because we didn't have the money to give them more and they don't understand that.

Alex Bruno: The farmers uh huh —

Dame Eugenia: But at least, for instant the Carib Reserve has never had a feeder road before we gave them two (2) feeder roads.

We went and look for water for the Carib Reserve. Well I refuse to take the water from the river because it would be dirty all the time, I wanted water from above but -and also I wanted that it wasn't water surrounding agricultural land so people could spray in the water catchment you know.

Alex Bruno: So until such time you couldn't give Carib Reserve water?

Dame Eugenia: We found a place and we were looking at it and we were going to join it with the water um… thing in Marigot and Wesley. But you know you have a plan, you do it, but you don't get the money for it right away so it takes time to put it in, because you don't have the money yourself. You have to go and look for the money from somebody else.

Alex Bruno: It appears like the Caribs are very

happy and they said for the first time in five hundred years they got —

Dame Eugenia: That is what the government party is telling you, for the first five hundred years you getting water but the Caribs are not saying that. Now ask them. They were very disappointed with the program. It's being done so badly, and they are criticizing it.

Alex Bruno: The Gallion people?

Dame Eugenia: The people... I don't know if Gallion people in it but no - Gallion when we did there, we had to re-do the water in Soufriere it was badly done and Gallion people wanted a road and they wanted water. I told them they can't have both. We don't have the money for both, choose which one you want and we will do that one for you. And they said we rather have the road because we can carry water up to our place in a tank, so we rather have the road so we can go up with it, and we want the road to take our things to market. So we got the money for the road we didn't have the money ourselves, we begged people for it and we got it from the FAO and when we were - opened the road we were down in - sitting down in Soufriere, and some of the people who were a group of people on the road, said only a thousand people there what you putting a road up there for them for? I said they have to take their carrots to market to sell so they have to have a road to do it. That's why they putting the road.

Alex Bruno: Dame, you got involved in a number of things and this program is going to really highlight and to even clear um, a number of charges you might have gotten; the name 'Iron Lady' can you tell us how exactly how you got that name?

Dame Eugenia: I don't know. They'd called Mrs. Thatcher the Iron Lady, in Britain, and they thought that I was just as troublesome as she was, so they called me the 'Iron Lady' too.

Alex Bruno: Troublesome meaning?

Dame Eugenia: That what, when I wanted something I pester people until I got it you know, because I couldn't have got the things I got if I hadn't been asking people abroad for it you know, because we didn't have any money ourselves you know. Everything we wanted we had to go and get the money from somebody abroad, so you had to have a good plan; people had to see where you were going to benefit the citizens not yourself, and it had to be - you had to have the capacity to do what you want to do in the plan.

Alex Bruno: So you not a hard, wicked bourgeois?

Dame Eugenia: I'm not a bourgeois at all. My father was a peasant my mother was a peasant. The both of them went to elementary school, but they taught me that other people have a right to have their point of view and you must listen to that too. Even In our house, everybody had their point of view.

Alex Bruno: Do you remember the events of the military disturbances in Grenada?

Dame Eugenia: Oh yes…uh-hmm. There was, there was…what was - the plans that were being made in Grenada were frightening to rest of the Caribbean because we felt that they would knock off each of us after a time and you know take over in each place.

Alex Bruno: What was happening tell us because -

Dame Eugenia: Well, the Grenada government had - first of all they had thrown out the elected government - not by an election, they had done it forcefully and I'm against that. I think it must have law and order where ever you are. Then – because otherwise I would have been trying to throw out the UWP by now, but let them ruin the country and ruin themselves and let people see for themselves they are not fit to run the country and let…the people themselves will throw them out - and then, so… but they were and they, in fact there were things that we didn't know, but they were really were…they had thrown out the government and they'd taken over and in fact they um the communists, in fact, were taking over in that aspect. And it wasn't only in Grenada you know, every island they had formed a group to do it. And when we were in London we knew that, from when I was a student in London I saw it happening. There were people who lived in the same residence with me who were the agents of the communist party and, we knew that. In fact, I remember one place we lived in an old house, and the stairs squeaked and we know which stair squeaked and we would jump it so the person, so the agent who was at the top of the stairs wouldn't hear us because otherwise he would be dragging us in to talk to us.

So and I mean I, I'm not inclined to be communist because I think everybody must have their say they must open their mouth, they must talk they must explain what they want. I think everybody has a right to that and so I was opposed to what was happening. But that wasn't my business if Grenada wanted to run their business that way, but I was afraid if Grenada became really part and parcel of it that we would not be ready when it happens to us. We had a meeting here in August, I think it was woman, Caribbean or OECS Caribbean women in the OECS, and all the heads of state in the OECS had come. Mr. Bishop had booked his room, had send down two soldiers to stand guard at his room before he came down you know - I'm living at my home no guard living here - the only guard in the hotel room. He arrived the morning, he left the afternoon so he never slept in the room. I don't think he ever saw the room and he came - I had arranged to have lunch, a different lunch everyday so that the heads could talk together closely, and in his case, when I um - when he came to visit me, he arrived in the morning and he left in the afternoon so he didn't require the guards he had in his room. But he asked me, he told me I would like you to speak to the Americans for me 'cause I've just been to America and they have ignored me completely. They didn't give me any listening. And I had spoken to Cord because Cord was minister of finance and I use to meet him at the World bank meetings, and I said why do you come here to ask for help why don't you go to your friends in the East and leave us to get what is available here in the West for us who are on the West side, and he said you think they give you money? Those people they only make promises you know they never give you anything you know. So I said what you sticking with them for it they don't give you anything? But anyway, it was what bothered us after thing when um, Morris Bishop was put in the house arrest by his people, the Caribbean people spoke and said they should think intervene. I said no. It is true he is not an elected government but the people have accepted him as if elected and if the people want to put him under house arrest that is their business not ours. We can't interfere in Grenada's business. If they wanted him under house arrest I'm not going to interfere. They must decide for themselves what they want. So, but then when, we had a meeting, we were having a meeting with CARICOM in Trinidad and so all of us in the small islands have to pass through Barbados to go Trinidad, so whilst we were there, we had a meeting among ourselves and for the first time I saw Caribbean people who immediately said we've got to go, we've got to get rid of what's happening there. And we got word from the Governor General who was the only person in position there but he was under house arrest, and he had sent word to us both by the British Assistant Commissioner and the

Venezuelans who had visited him, that we must do something. He didn't tell us what we must do but we must do something, so we decided we should go in but we knew. I was the one who could give - I was going to give ten people going from the army that I had. The others were going to give five and four, we didn't have enough among ourselves. So… and that next day there was a newscast that the top army brass in Cuba had gone to Grenada, so we decided we had to ask the larger country to help us, so, went to America and ask them for help. They would send men down to help us to free Grenada. By that time that they had killed three of ministers already.

Alex Bruno: I understood what um brought… so Bishop and his people by force took over the –

Dame Eugenia: There was no election they just took over government from Gairy. Now I know, look I had no sympathy for Eric Gairy.

Dame Eugenia: I think if he had been a better leader, Bishop would not have the sympathy of the people.

Alex Bruno: Why did Bishop take over?

Dame Eugenia: Because people were disagreeing with what Gairy was doing and what he was doing, and what he was saying, as we were disagreeing with Patrick here.

Alex Bruno: But Dame, you I was told was leader of the OECS then?

Dame Eugenia: Yes, I was chairman of the OECS I was the one who had to speak on their behalf.

Alex Bruno: So you called in the Americans?

Dame Eugenia: No, we agreed to call the

Americans but we were going to Trinidad and we came back from Trinidad and had not gotten answer from the Americans yet. We came back with the ambassador we knew in Barbados, and he had not got the reply yet because the president was somewhere in the south, in the southern states playing golf, so I decided that I wanted to go up and talk to them because I don't think they realized how serious it was for us.

Alex Bruno: What year was that…1983?

Dame Eugenia: Yes, 1983. So I went to - I came back here and I called as soon as I got to the airport I called Barbados and I said if I can get through on the air, because the telephone never use to work in the airport. I waited until I got an omen that I could go ahead with the idea that we have. So I went - I called Barbados and I told them you have a plane there from the States I'd like a lift to Washington when you passing you pick me up. He said we can't come to Dominica your airport is too small, I said I know but you can go into Guadeloupe and I will arrange for you to land in Guadeloupe and I will go to Guadeloupe to meet you there. So we did that and that's how I went to America.

Alex Bruno: Dame Eugenia there was stories, and I believe it is written, I'm not sure if it's in your book the, 'Iron Lady', or somebody else publication that you might have received on behalf of the people of the Caribbean, one hundred thousand dollars ($100,000)?

Dame Eugenia: I wish we had. I would have more than that if one hundred thousand wouldn't have gone very far among all those islands but they keep saying so but it's not so.

But if I'd gotten a hundred thousand dollars and put it in the bank here, don't you think everybody would know that? It would sink the bank with so much money at one time you know what I mean. So everybody would have known that. It wouldn't be a secret anymore.

Alex Bruno: Things starting changing in the 80s for the party. The party seemingly started fragmenting in the late 80s early 90s?

Dame Eugenia: I don't they were fragmenting; I think we stayed together pretty well.

Alex Bruno: There was the leadership run that was —

Dame Eugenia: When I was - I decided that I was going and I wanted to have somebody in my place before I left so I ask them to choose a leader to take my place.

I was going to stay 'till the election date but they must have somebody who could take over for me and run the party and there was nothing wrong in that. I thought it was a good idea instead of just leaving and then having them to look for somebody then. So, they had an election. What I think was that I didn't expect there to be so much competition for it. I didn't think - but they didn't realize that it wasn't a nice job to do, nobody want to do it but they… there was only one person interested in it, and there were more than one group of people interested in it putting people that they wanted in it.

Alex Bruno: That broke up the party?

Dame Eugenia: Not really. There was an- it was an election and they um, and Alleyne won and there was no difficulty about that. We accepted that we - it was a fair election.

Everybody was there to cast their vote and he won and that was fine as far as the reference said.

Alex Bruno: Do you ever remember making public statements to the fact that Alleyne Carbon was still your man?

Dame Eugenia: No, no, no I never said so, I didn't say that. Well they know I voted for Carbon. I didn't hesitate. Everybody had a right to vote where they wanted and I thought that Carbon - well you know they said always calling us bourgeois party and I thought if Carbon was leader of the party they wouldn't call us bourgeois you know. Also Carbon was a very good minister. He knew his work, he followed his work carefully, he ran a good department and he knew people. He knew people better than I knew them you know, because he used to drive up and down Portsmouth everyday pick up people on the way and talk to them you know what I mean? So I thought he would have been a good leader because - and he would have come from humble people and they would have preferred it you know.

Alex Bruno: I was told that this election was the straw that broke the camel's back?

Dame Eugenia: Who is that?

Alex Bruno: Leadership election within the party and the fragmentation caused the party –

Dame Eugenia: Well, I think that too many ran. I mean I didn't think that was going to be that eagerness to take over the job of leadership because it's such a hard job, but there were four (4) people around ran I think they were. Naturally the party divided among the four.

They wouldn't have run if they haven't had support. So you had a small party with four different factions looking for leadership.

Alex Bruno: Hence the dismal showing at the last election?

Dame Eugenia: Not really. I think that the um… I don't think it was because of that we didn't win. People get tired of you, you know. They see you there for fifteen years… it's time to get - let's get new face and a new idea and new things. People get tired and they want something new and that's what caused it, I think. We've been there for fifteen years and people were tired.

Alex Bruno: Since your retirement…there is, there has been another new leader because I mean Alleyne left the scene half-way I mean just after, I'm not sure why he left I don't know if you want to comment on that?

Dame Eugenia: He was offered the job as a judge and you can't blame him. He is a lawyer and to be a judge is a good thing you know, so that's a good position to be in. Also it's a way in which you can really serve your country well too.

Alex Bruno: Savarin is now in charge?

Dame Eugenia: Uh huh, he is the leader and he was elected by the people you know, he was, the party elected him he wasn't just put there you know. The Party elected him and without opposition he was elected.

Alex Bruno: You remain a member of the party and you are proud of your present leadership?

Dame Eugenia: Yes, I think so, and I think that Savarin understands the problem of small people. You know having been a leader of the civil service, he understands the needs of people who are small income area, and what must be done to help them to be able to succeed in life you know.

Alex Bruno: So, when people say that he was given the position as Ambassador at large, to…in Britain the UN, when you- Europe- when you won that's some pay off for the hard work, he done for you?

Dame Eugenia: No, no, no because I wanted a person who could stand up for us and he did a very good job for us. Bananas would have gone long ago if it hadn't been for him. He did an excellent job for us when he was looking after our banana thing. He was well respected by the people, other people from around the world who had the banana you know.

Alex Bruno: Dame Eugenia you are about one of the

very best persons who can speak and analyze the situation right now politically in Dominica, Savarin leader, Edison James and we have Rosie…

Dame Eugenia: I don't see how anybody can vote for Edison James. I consider he's inept. I consider he doesn't understand anything that is happening around him and he doesn't try to understand and he is not interested in Dominicans and where they are going.

Alex Bruno: Rosie —

Dame Eugenia: I really condemn Edison James as one of the worst leaders we ever had in Dominica.

Alex Bruno: Really?

Dame Eugenia: Uh huh.

Alex Bruno: Rosie Douglas?

Dame Eugenia: Rosie Douglas not interested in Dominica because he flying all over the world talking to other people. He is more interested in looking after the affairs of other countries than he looking after our country.

Alex Bruno: People say he have never worked. Have he really never worked?

Dame Eugenia: No, he never worked, uh huh.

Alex Bruno: So how does he get his money?

Dame Eugenia: I suppose through his family. I don't know.

Alex Bruno: You're a diplomat you know, (*laughs*). Tell me about Savarin?

Dame Eugenia: Savarin has worked all his life he was a civil servant, he was a teacher and he worked very well, he was extremely good for the job he did in Brussels for us.

He was highly respected by all of the countries who had to deal with him because he knew what was happening. He could voice his opinion and he wasn't afraid to state what he thought, and I - that's important in a leader. You mustn't be a afraid to say what you believe in.

Alex Bruno: Be quite frank with me. Tell me who do you see wining that election in terms of what you feel going on?

Dame Eugenia: I think that he will win. I think that the Freedom Party will win. You know the government party is making a lot of noise now and we think from what they saying that they've already won the election, but there are a lot of people who decides that, and they will pay and they said that they have a million dollars to pay for votes and knowing Dominicans

I presume they would accept the money. I told them – they - accept it it's yours. If they have a million dollars to pay for votes is because they made the money on your head, so you must take the money that they giving you, but you must not vote for them because they wouldn't have a million dollars next election again, when they finish ruining the country.

Alex Bruno: Dame, you are very strong for your age, I mean not that you are advanced I believe that you are well lived –

Dame Eugenia: I am eighty years old so it's time to get out and relax.

Alex Bruno: There are people at eighty now starting government as you would know. Wouldn't you love some public office with the president or something?

Dame Eugenia: No, no, no. I wouldn't want the

president for anything, and I said that if the government had asked me to be an ambassador abroad for them, I would have accepted it, because I would be working for Dominica still, but of course they wouldn't agree with my opinion and I wouldn't agree with theirs so I could never be their ambassador. An ambassador must express what they think and I don't think that they have any good thoughts and I wouldn't be expressing what they think.

Alex Bruno: If they would call you now, Dame, and offer you the job to be Ambassador at large wouldn't you take the job?

Dame Eugenia: On conditions that they understand that I would not just follow them blindly. I will give them ideas of what should be done. I will tell then what the situation is and if they don't want to put those things together and come up with a plan that can help Dominica I'll just get out, cause I'm not in any job except I can help Dominica with it you know.

Alex Bruno: And would you still remain aligned to the Freedom Party then?

Dame Eugenia: Oh yes, I wouldn't do a thing; I think the Freedom Party has more sense than the other two parties. I think the Freedom Party is interested in the little person in Dominica and I think that is the important thing about the Freedom Party.

Alex Bruno: But if five years ago people were fed up sort of as you said in your words of the Freedom Party, why now five years after they would be again interested in the party? Because they've been so let down by this government and they don't see any hope that Rosie is going to take life seriously as a politician.

That is why. So let's go back to what we already knew, they've looked after us well in the past. Dame, speaking with you gave me a lot of revelation that you're just not the person that sometimes you hear about. I haven't really met you before a couple of years and spoken with you, and I find you so very pleasant. What about your personality you believe sort of distracted the so call less fortunate?

Dame Eugenia: Well, people just think that. They were told and you know people listen to what they were told, they were told that I was rich and didn't care about the poor. But it was not true that I was rich, I didn't complain about the fact that I wasn't rich. I manage to live on what I had. I didn't have to cry about it, you know so Williams the minister of communications always saying about they not going to leave government poor like the Freedom party am ministers did, but you don't go into government to make money for yourself. You go into government to make life better for the people whom you are serving.

Dame Eugenia: You are the servant of the people and your job is to look after their welfare, to their benefit and to listen to what they have to say too because *'tout cachil parka waytey en un tete' ('the ability to think does not reside in one person's head')*. You have to know that other people have ideas which you must look at and listen to and see how to adapt them to the things to be done.

Alex Bruno: You served for fifteen years, and you still serving Dominica through and we have touched that until now. Tell us about the Foundation that you involve with -

Dame Eugenia: Well, I knew... I told you my parents only had elementary school education but there was always - knew us children that we were going to have higher school education. We were going to have professions we were going to go university. Nobody ever told you so in so many words but you were being pushed along the way, so you're studied and you fitted yourself to be able to go further and so I realized education was what my father was worth. My father had actually no education; he went to primary school he went to the Roseau Boys School. My mother the same she only went to primary school. But importantly, they believed in education. They felt that education is important, that is what they imbued us their children with now most of what I have is something that my father earned. I haven't got any property in my name. I've never had property in my own name; well, all the property was in a company that my father and I formed.

Alex Bruno: What was the Company –

Dame Eugenia: JB Charles and Company. But now that I formed the Foundation, I formed the JB Charles foundation, I'm selling the property and the money is going into the foundation. It's from that money I'm using interest on that money - I'm using to mind the scholarships I'm giving.

Alex Bruno: So, when was the JB Charles foundation formed and um what amount of property do you have to sell?

Dame Eugenia: Well, I have the house I use to live in before, and there was six acres of land there by different lots and I think I had three or four more to sell (coughs) and the thing, the important thing is –

Alex Bruno: When did you establish the foundation?

Dame Eugenia: Oh… I think perhaps two years after I left government. I was already giving scholarships but I hadn't registered the foundation, and…and I really want to do it in honor of my father because he was a man who had no education, he believed in education and he did a lot for people. There are a lot of people he helped. Every time a person won an island scholarship, he found that person and gave them some pocket money to use when they went and, study because he thought it was important. And so I want to be able to use his money for that purpose, to make sure that people have an education. So, I'm not using any of the money for myself. I mean people think I am rich, but I never was rich and I'm not rich now. I'm living on my pension and the pension is small – as Mr.

Williams keeps saying that he is not so stupid as to leave government as poor as the Freedom Party Ministers, but I didn't go to government to make money, I went into government there to make Dominica a better place for Dominicans to live in.

Alex Bruno: You got a lot of things, some perks and incentives as a result of helping Dominicans; don't you think?

Dame Eugenia: But I only got it for Dominica. I did not get it for myself. I did not get paid anything for myself.

Alex Bruno: Such as Dame Eugenia, the title?

Dame Eugenia: But that doesn't bring any money with it. It's a name, fine, and it does more good for - I took it because I believe it does more good for Dominica to know that somebody, the leader of our small country was appreciated by people bigger than us you know.

Alex Bruno: While you were in government, didn't you get some contacts and establish new friendships, or got some –

Dame Eugenia: I made friends, but I did not make friends who were going to help me economically.

Alex Bruno: You were not better off when you came out of government than when you got in?

Dame Eugenia: No, no, I was worse off! I was making good money as a lawyer before I went into government.

Alex Bruno: If you had to do it again, would you spend the fifteen –

Dame Eugenia: Because I think I made - I changed some things in Dominica that required changing, and I intend, until I die, to keep on making sure that there are changes in Dominica for the benefit of Dominicans on a whole.

Alex Bruno: For the people who think you are 80, so you should shut up and relax yourself, what do you have to advise them?

Dame Eugenia: Well, I not dead yet, I telling them. When I dead, my mouth will be shut, but whilst I'm alive, and I see things, I have a right to talk about them. I'm paying taxes still!

Alex Bruno: The way I see it, you will be speaking for a long, long, long time again, Dame…(*laughs*)

Dame Eugenia: But I think it is necessary for people who have the right to talk; to talk on how they see things, and to talk about these things. You know, for instance, the French gave us a lot of help I told you, medically, health wise. Do you know that it is only a couple months ago, a few months ago that Edison went, Edison visited Guadeloupe? And that is where the basis of this friendship comes, so I think you must keep your friends to help you. You don't have to do it only because they help you, but you have to learn to live with them because, in fact, they do give you assistance. I mean, when I asked the British to give us the water front in Roseau, I also ask them to give us a cruise ship berth, and the British said no, two million pounds and no more. I didn't quarrel, it was their money; I was not entitled to it. So, I went to the French and I tell the French the British are going to fix our water front, how about a little Anglo-Franco arrangement, and you do the cruise ship berth for us nah? They came and they did it, and some people are earning a living as a result of the cruise ship berth. So, I don't see why you shouldn't, I should…

more should be done, we are not selling enough, we are not preparing enough things, and I have some skilled and working people to make that we could sell to the tourist, because that's where you make the money.

Alex Bruno: What kind of awards you received in your time?

Dame Eugenia: I received a lot of university degrees. I don't remember them; South Carolina, Clemson, Harvard – all of these have given me awards, but I don't boast about that; I don't talk about it –

Alex Bruno: You have to; you have to do that now because I mean we are going to feature you. So, how can we know about them?

Dame Eugenia: I have to look them up, because I don't remember all of them. The University of the West Indies has given me one, and the University of South Carolina, and I got help, and you know, I go to a university and they would offer me a degree and I would tell them I would much rather if you allow degrees to the little people who cannot afford to come to your university.

Dame Eugenia: Why won't you give them a scholarship instead? I would appreciate that more, and I got a lot of scholarships for people that way. They would go and study at the expense of the university because the university wanted to recognized me.

Alex Bruno: Are you going to go on to do a doctorate some time?

Dame Eugenia: No, no, no, I'm finished studying. I'm relaxing. I'm enjoying my easy life now.

Alex Bruno: You haven't had the highest award of Dominica bestowed on you –

Dame Eugenia: Oh, they won't give me an award.

This government would never give me an award. I would never give an award to myself. When I was in government, I could have given myself an award, but you don't give yourself an award you know. The government will never give me one; this government will never give me an award! So, I'm not - and award don't mean a thing to me you know – quite frankly. I was appreciative of the one the Queen gave me because I like the Queen. And every time I went to a meeting of CARICOM, a Commonwealth meeting, every leader had an interview with the Queen, a 20 minute interview, and I always looked forward to that, because she was so knowledgeable about what was happening in those countries, and so I appreciate the fact that she gave me an award. I took it as an honor to Dominica more than to myself you know.

Alex Bruno: We… almost winding down, but I know it might be a little taxing because there are a lot of things you have done for Dominica already, in terms of government, can you tell me a number of achievements that you might have…

Dame Eugenia: The roads! That was a very important thing, and it was done so well, supported by the World Bank, and you know we would have had that airport; you know that. The British were prepared to do it for us. They came down, they did the study and decided where it should go; the cost of it, and few people would have lost their land. But, *(inaudible)*… would have lost some of their land which now belongs to chairman of the present party; Bioche would have lost some of his land next door, and the nuns would have lost a part of their land where they have the Convent up there. But the rest, the other people would not have lost their land. The school would not have been interfered with at all – the school they have at Marigot; the secondary school, and we would have had the airport. But you know that – in a way it is because I wanted more; I wanted more money for feeder roads. The amount of money the British was going to spend, I told them I would like some of it to go to feeder roads, because if we had an airport, I wanted the farmer to ship his goods out and we must have roads to take these things to the airport. And the British – so I went to the Americans and ask them if they would join with the British to do the airport for us, because then there would be money released from the British to do the feeder roads, and the Americans came down – they looked at it. I asked them for that, and I also asked them for a road which would take us closer to the boiling lake – not right to the shore, but to the top where you could look down to the boiling lake, and then you would have the path to the boiling lake where more energetic people would walk down, but older people could go at the top, drive and sit there and look at the boiling lake. So, I wanted that, and the British – the Americans came and they studied both and they said they preferred to do the airport, and they were prepared to come and do the work for us. They would have come with their corps of engineers, and I said you must employ some of our people who had heavy equipment, so they could learn from working with you all how to become more efficient. And this is what was planned, but Edison wrote the Americans urging them not to help us with the airport, because it was not right that we had the airport. It was an election stunt they said, but if we had the airport, two elections would have passed there, the airport would have there you know; it does not go in the election box and throw it away. Anyway, he stopped the airport. He told the Americans he did not want them coming into his country, because you know, even if he's not the leader of the country, he is the leader of a party so the Americans would not come. Because if something happens to one of their soldiers, they would have been blamed for not taking the warning of a leader in the country.

Alex Bruno: Don't you think that is a lot of power from, I mean that one letter?

Dame Eugenia: It wasn't power; it was, he was the head of a party. He was the head of the opposition party and he told them that elections were coming up, and I was just doing that - I was using them for election purposes. I don't require any airport; the airport was not necessary – he completely kibosh it! And now, the same thing he kibosh, he's killing himself trying to get, and he's not going to get it, you know that. The British, why didn't he go to the British and ask them? The British already had the plans, they would have continued and given it to him. The same way – the road to Delice, the British had agreed to give me that road. I had taken the minister there, he'd seen it and I had asked for a school at Grand Bay from the British, and I said I want the secondary school at Grand Bay so the people from that district could drive down to school there, but you must give me the road. And they were going to give us the road; they had planned it and all. But they told me it was a very difficult road to do. I said difficult or not, get it done!

So, but he didn't - so he didn't want us to get this help from the British. So, he stopped the Americans coming and told them that it was not a good thing because it was close to elections and that I was doing for election purposes, so naturally that would put off the Americans.

Alex Bruno: I think he would be happy to hear you saying that, he would think he is as strong man now.

Dame Eugenia: Well, he may think he's strong but he is the leader of a party, and if you tell the Americans that their people will be in danger if they come here at that time, they are going to listen you know, because they don't know who is going to do the danger; if is he going to do the danger –

Alex Bruno: Did his letter; his letter said that?

Dame Eugenia: Oh yes, that if they sent their

soldiers, they would be in danger, and so they should not come.

Alex Bruno: Can we get a copy of the letter anywhere?

Dame Eugenia: I published it the other day in The Chronicle, and I hear that mister…minister of finance now; I was in Washington at the… the World Bank had invited me. It was after I had retired from politics, from government. So, Mr. Timothy told them that I had come to this meeting, World Bank meeting, to tell them that I do not want an international airport. Timothy actually said those words. But now he is writing to the Americans telling them that they should give them the help to build the international airport. So, I hear – if it's true, I haven't seen that letter – so I hear that the Americans sent them back, sent him back, a photostat copy of Edison's letter to them, written in my time, saying we shouldn't have an international airport.

Alex Bruno: So, the airport is a no no? it is not going to be built?

Dame Eugenia: No, I don't think they going to get the money to build it. Where are they going to get the money from? They haven't asked the British who would have given it to them. They told the Americans that they mustn't - that they don't want the international airport – all the Americans were there when Timothy spoke about that. So, I don't think we will get the international airport. And quite frankly, if, we have been asking the American airlines to send in their Eagle there when we were in government, and if they had agreed to do that before we had left government, I probably would not bother about an international airport. I would have wanted to buy an Eagle plane and let the

American airlines run it for us. So, you could have two flights a day – you know – one flight a day.

Alex Bruno: Why wasn't Rosie and Saverin, and Athie Martin to great extent, able to stop the project as is right now in terms of the letters and the protests that they have done and, and –

Dame Eugenia: They have! You see anybody coming forward to give them money to build the airport? Not even they are pretending that they are getting money to build the airport you know. They say that Taiwanese give them so much money on condition that their plans are in order; the Taiwanese have never given us money on any condition before. Why is it that they have put a condition, because they don't think the government is ready to do any airport, that's why.

Alex Bruno: You don't think Dominica needs that airport.

Dame Eugenia: No, no. I think that you can do without it now because you have these connections; because having an international airport won't bring the British planes to Dominica you know, because the new style of doing, running airport business is to have hubs. You want a hub in St. Lucia for Dominica from Britain and that sort of thing. I mean, I have no problem, you know, leaving here and going to America; I go to American every two months for a meeting. I get on Eagle, get to Puerto Rico, walk across the floor to get the plane to go to America. It's easy.

Alex Bruno: How does someone get to, (I'm going back to your Fund), to be chosen or to be se –

Dame Eugenia: You have to write and say – first of all you have to get entrance into university; I'm not doing that for you. You have to decide what you want to study, and you have to get entrance into university to study, and when you get that letter, then you must send it to me and ask me for help. And if I am satisfied that what you are going to study is going to be worthwhile for Dominica, I will write you and say, okay – I will write the university and say, okay, and I will… I will help you, but if I think that what you are going to study is not worth a damn in Dominica, I'm not. I just telling sorry, I can't assist you.

Alex Bruno: Will your funds run short some time?

Dame Eugenia: Well, I have the – my money is invested in the bank. Not in an offshore bank; I don't, I'm not, I am afraid of those.

I don't know enough of them. So, I like a bank that's known and steady, and I get the interest of it every month, and it's that interest I am using.

Alex Bruno: That would have been a substantial amount of money, Dame Eugenia. I mean, it's not, it's not cheap at all to –

Dame Eugenia: Well, it cost, it cost; each student cost about fourteen thousand dollars a year, but you only pay a term at a time – two terms. I don't pay the summer term. I tell them before hand; no summer term, and the students must come back to Dominica to work.

Alex Bruno: How many –

Dame Eugenia: You must pay the money. When they come back, they have to pay the money back. I am not going to send people to go and work, to qualify for the Americans.

	We require them qualified here in Dominica.
Alex Bruno:	They pay the money back to you?
Dame Eugenia:	Yes. If they - when they come back, they must come back to Dominica to work, and when they come, begin to work, they must pay the money back -
Alex Bruno:	So, it's a loan… a grant -
Dame Eugenia:	It's a loan, but if the person doesn't come back, and I give permission for them to work abroad, they don't have to pay the money back. I really want the money to continue so that more people can study, you know.
Alex Bruno:	So, it's not really a scholarship; it's a fund –
Dame Eugenia:	It's a foundation; a fund.
Alex Bruno:	Dame Eugenia, we winding down

on this part of the interview; tell me what has been the most, single, greatest achievement you have had as a person?

Dame Eugenia: I don't think I had any great achievements. I've just managed to exist all these years and let Dominica continue to exist. And I think it is important, that in spite of Patrick's planning against the country, we were able to continue and make the country live in spite of his attempts to knock it down.

Alex Bruno: Why have you been a great person?

Dame Eugenia: I'm not. I don't think I am. Nobody ask me you know, if I was great. I just heard outside. You know, they didn't write and tell me you've been chosen as a great person and the others chosen with you know.

Dame Eugenia: If they had just told me, I'd

written back to them, personally, and tell them if they are going to put Patrick John as a great person, take me out. I don't want to be in the list. Because I do not see how you can make Patrick a great person with what he did to the country.

Alex Bruno: The people who seem to think that, um, you was one of the persons who assisted in breeding this, what we call, hate, because of what you say about Patrick on the radio publicly, or how would you defend that? I mean —

Dame Eugenia: I don't. I mean, the people who live in Dominica and like Patrick, like Patrick. Those who know that, in fact, he did harm to the country don't like him, and I am one of those who know he did harm to the country.

Alex Bruno: Dame Eugenia, you chose not to have ever gotten married or to make a child; any particular reason?

Dame Eugenia: No, I didn't meet anybody I wanted to leave home for. I was - my parents were very good to me and kept me very happy at home. So, I didn't require to look for any other company. And that's why.

Alex Bruno: I remember, on the occasion – it believe it was your…it would have been, I'm not sure whether it was your sixtieth birthday, there was a big bash for you as the mother of the nation, and there was some controversy about you not having a child so how can you become a mother?

Dame Eugenia: I didn't become a mother of a child, I became a mother of the nation because I was interested in what happen to the country, and was looking out for the best for the country and that is why they called me that. I don't know that I am the mother of the nation but I believe in Dominica, I believe that Dominica has a lot of good in it and there are a lot of good people in it, and we must make sure that these people triumph and, therefore, keep Dominica good.

Alex Bruno: As a matter of fact, you are. You feel as if, you feel that you have been a mother and you are still a mother –

Dame Eugenia: Uh huh. I still think there are things that I can do for the country, and I intend to continue doing them, because I think Dominica is important.

Alex Bruno: Dame Eugenia, there are a lot of things that we can do. Um… and a lot of things that we can say. And I have asked you a number of questions that you have answered quite frankly.

I mean, you have been honest with us and we are very happy that you have been that way. But if there is something that you could have changed in your life? What would that have been, or what would that be?

Dame Eugenia: I would wish the we would never had a Patrick John…doing harm to our country and giving our country a bad name. I couldn't do anything about that. His mother give birth to him, and it's not his mother's fault that he turned out that way, because his mother was a very good woman; I knew her well. She was a huckster and I used to supply her. I used to drive to her home to deliver oranges and grapefruits to her from our estate, so I know she was a good person.

Alex Bruno: Who change Patrick; who spoilt Patrick?

Dame Eugenia: Patrick couldn't take power. He thought that once he was in government he could say and do what he liked. That, you know, he was important.

Dame Eugenia: I have never thought that I was important because I was head of government, but he thought so and that thought spoilt him. He, he spoilt himself.

Alex Bruno: Who was the most powerful states-person you worked with in the past?

Dame Eugenia: You mean, in Dominica? (*pause*) I don't know, I think the members of my cabinet were the ones that I admired. People like Maynard and Brian Alleyne, um, and especially, the man who died in the north, Alleyne Carbon – he was a good man. He understood people, he knew people and he was interested in the welfare of people.

Alex Bruno: What would you have liked to do for Dominica that you hadn't gotten the chance to do?

Dame Eugenia: I would like to get more investment in Dominica so there would be more jobs, and I don't mean offshore banks. I really mean, I would like to see, I would have like to have had factories as we had tried to do at um… (*inaudible*)- Belfast, Canefield, so there would be more work and persons would be able to hold their own in those jobs, you know.

Alex Bruno: Why have Leblanc maintain his silence over those years?

Dame Eugenia: I don't know… because he wasn't interested in the country. If he was interested in country, he couldn't keep silent when he saw things were going wrong. If you've worked in the country, you helped to build the country, if you see things going wrong, you cannot just sit back and let it happen. You must talk out if you find faults in the persons who are doing the wrong things.

Alex Bruno: What —

Dame Eugenia: I think that Leblanc was disappointed because he allowed Patrick to succeed him, and that's why he has kept silent. You remember there was a time when it felt that Armour would succeeded him? Um, Ronald Armour, and instead of that Patrick came in. I think Leblanc got disappointed then.

Alex Bruno: What is this —

Dame Eugenia: From that time, he kept his silence and stayed out of town. He did not come to Roseau.

Alex Bruno: Have you tried speaking with him since?

Dame Eugenia: No, I never tried.

Alex Bruno: Who is the most hated person that you know of –

Dame Eugenia: Nobody. I think people forgive people easily in Dominica. People don't carry grudges long in Dominica.

Alex Bruno: But you seem to hate, well you don't hate Patrick, but you seem to have something against him.

Dame Eugenia: Well, I dislike the fact that he was plotting with the Ku Klux Klan to take over the country for the purpose of putting drug factories in Dominica. That's what I was… am against. I think it was a wrong move. I think it was a wrong move. I think it was wrong to think of that for Dominica. That's not what Dominica was meant to be.

Alex Bruno: Dame Eugenia, if you had a

message now for Dominica; a short message, brief message, what would you tell the people –

Dame Eugenia: That people have to work together. That people have to understand that there will always be people who are better off and people who are not so well off, but that doesn't mean that there should be a dividing line between those people. Those people must get together and work together for the purpose of building a strong Dominica.

Alex Bruno: How do you see our country in the next like um two decades?

Dame Eugenia: Well, unless this is done – what I am saying there – if won't be different from what we are now.

Alex Bruno: What would you like us – as a generation – a nation, to do for you or for, um, your legacy and that of your family, generally.

Dame Eugenia: I would like people to realize that hard work never killed anybody; that you don't get anything unless you have hard work and good plans *(pause)* to, to work with. You don't just work hard; you work hard with good plans for the purpose of improving the lot of every single Dominican. I want every Dominican to be better off as a result of us having lived in this world.

Alex Bruno: Have you regretted anything in your life?

Dame Eugenia: No. I am perfectly happy. I was happy – I was glad that I went into government when I did. I am happy that I was able to do some things. I'm sorry that I didn't, I didn't have all the money I required to do all the things that were necessary. For instance, you know, the hospital – for instance – we had plan to do the new surgical ward.

The French came the other day and told me they can't understand that I was not invited in the, when they turned the ground there.

Dame Eugenia: I said why should I be invited? The government does not think I exist. They don't think I ever lived, so they wouldn't invite me. But they said without you they would have never got that; it was your project; you were the one who pushed it and made the French give it to you.

Alex Bruno: That had - they have invited you to a number of public things that you didn't –

Dame Eugenia: Not those things, no.

Alex Bruno: What about during independence?

Dame Eugenia: Well, they invited me to the parade, but I don't always go. It is early in the morning and I am in bed and sleeping.

I don't get up at seven any more...nowadays, that's the beauty of old age.

Alex Bruno: A number of people seemed to have made it besides you.

Dame Eugenia: Yes, but with old age, you can relax as you like; you don't have to go anywhere.

Alex Bruno: What apologies would you have to make? If any?

Dame Eugenia: That I wasn't able to get all the money that Dominicans required to put things in place for them; I regretted that. It isn't that I didn't try, but it is - wasn't everybody was there with an open hand to give it to you. So, I wish I'd had more money to do the things I planned to do. I would have had feeder roads in every corner of the island; I would have liked good roads in every corner of the island;

	I would have like good roads all over the island.
Alex Bruno:	When that time comes, which is quite inevitable for everyone to leave this earth, what are you going to leave with that you never told us about?
Dame Eugenia:	Nothing! I've told you everything. I've been frank and open and spoken from what I know, what I mean, and what I think, I haven't hidden anything, I have never been secretive about anything. I think when you are leading a country, that your thoughts and ideas are the peoples' ideas and thoughts and you must share them, and that's what I've done.
Alex Bruno:	Can you remember anything being done to you that you would have preferred not done in the way that it was done, or said about you?
Dame Eugenia:	*(long pause)*... Well a lot of things

they said about me was not true, so anything that was not true I would rather that it had not been said. I'd rather if people didn't manufacture things about me, but apart from that, no.

Alex Bruno: Which is the main –

Dame Eugenia: People have a right to have their opinion about me. Everybody can't like you.

Alex Bruno: Which is the main manufactured untruth about you that you want to dispel –

Dame Eugenia: That I am a very rich woman! That's very, that is a stupid, um, lie. That I am a very rich woman. If I was a rich woman, I would probably be living – like Rosie – I would probably be living in another country.

Alex Bruno: Is Rosie a rich man?

Dame Eugenia: Well, he certainly seems to travel well, and it costs you money to travel.

Alex Bruno: Should we investigate his travels?

Dame Eugenia: No, I don't think do. I don't think we - he is not in a position to get money from us, illegally, to travel.

Alex Bruno: So, where is he getting his money?

Dame Eugenia: Well, he has friends abroad who likes him and like to see him travel. There is no reason why he shouldn't, at least when he is abroad, I am sure he is talking about Dominica.

Alex Bruno: I would imagine. The younger generation coming up, um, can you enlighten them in any way –

Dame Eugenia: They don't know the history of Dominica, and they don't know – and unfortunately, this government thinks that the young generation must be given sport and fete, and that's all they require. I don't think so, I think the young generation must be taught to have principles, to be serious about life, to see that they are the builders of the future, and that they must put their all in it. I don't think it is enough to tell them: oh, you all can live on sport and fete; I don't agree with that.

Alex Bruno: Sports in terms of sports, and fete in terms of the enhance of the cultural; the Creole Music Festival and these things –

Dame Eugenia: I'm not against the enhancement on…that is happening; putting our culture o display. I am just saying that too much emphasis on that and not enough emphasis on people succeeding in building themselves and their country and their family.

Alex Bruno: How do you build your country?

Dame Eugenia: By building your family first, and by putting first things first.

Alex Bruno: Jamaicans did it with sports and music and culture, why can't we?

Dame Eugenia: Have they built their country? Would you like to go and live in Jamaica now with all the problems they have there- I don't think so? I'm not saying you mustn't have fete and sports; I am just saying it should not be the main reason for existence.

Alex Bruno: Generally, you believe that you would have done your best, and if anybody needs advice and help, they could come to you at any time?

Dame Eugenia: I would be glad to give them any advice I know that I can give them. They would have to express their point of view…you know.

Alex Bruno: I know one such person and, it's a

fact. He's a friend of mine. Branka, Senator Branka John. Branka John told me that he is praying one day to meet with you so that you could impart some of your knowledge into him –

Dame Eugenia: He is quite a good man, I think. He is a pleasant person, for one thing, he doesn't have that bouwé face that most of the leaders of the UWP have. He looks as if he is pleasant and enjoys life.

Alex Bruno: Can I tell him that he could come to see you?

Dame Eugenia: Anytime! I would be quite glad to talk to him.

Alex Bruno: Well, Dame Eugenia I am happy that you talked with us, and I know we will do justice to your story, and I'm looking forward to doing some other time with you –

Dame Eugenia: Don't call me a famous person.

I don't think I'm famous. I worked in Dominica. People know me because I worked in Dominica, and I am going to continue to work in Dominica. I think Dominica is my first love –

Alex Bruno: And only love?

Dame Eugenia: I think so.

Alex Bruno: You are married to Dominica.

Dame Eugenia: *(laughs).*

Alex Bruno: Dame Eugenia, thanks again.

Dame Eugenia: Okay…

End of interview.

Conclusion

Lasting legacy

Legends should have lasting legacies, but not everyone who has a lasting legacy is a legend. A legend, in the context of this book, is someone who is notoriously known, and widely acclaimed for a particular achievement. Legends are those who pass down unique and progressive aspects of life to other generations, so fame alone cannot be seen as legendary. If this were the case, Adolf Hitler would be one of the world's most celebrated legends.

In this book, the term lasting legacy refers to a solitary act, or series of actions and/or achievements which have unmistakably changed the order of things in a way that cannot be redone, nor can it/they, be totally reformed or undone. In that sense, let us look at the administrative achievements and other issues which Dame Eugenia have been engaged with, that:

1. Have unmistakably changed or altered the order of things in the Dominican community (or elsewhere)

2. Cannot be redone, or

3. Cannot be totally reformed.

It is important to state that Mary Eugenia Charles was Dominica's first female lawyer and Prime Minister. These titles, or achievements do not however count towards her lasting legacy, although they are historic.
I venture further to say that Eugenia was certainly a trailblazer in the field of law and politics, who later rose to prominence with her advocacy, administrative initiatives,

governing policies and political actions. This claim is made on the premise that one could be iconic, historic, memorable, remarkable, pioneering, with trailing-blazing valor, and may have had landmark achievements, but that person may not necessarily be legendary. That point has already been made, but to add another layer of clarity, to be a legend in any field of endeavor, one should have had accomplished a feat that no other person will ever be able to achieve, and not simply being the first to accomplish that goal. Case in point, Gordon Henderson is the legendary artiste, who, together with the other members of the Exile One band, created Dominica's Calypso, Cadence-Lypso in 1973.

Gordon, then, is a Cadence-Lypso legend. This means that no one else will ever be the creator of that genre of music, nor can Gordon's work be undone and/or totally reformed. Cadence-Lypso is Cadency-Lypso, even if new genres emerge. By my working definition, Gordon Henderson is a legend, and individuals like Phillip "Chubby" Mark and Marcel "Co" Mark of the Midnight Groovers, Jeff Joseph of Grammacks and others who placed their mark on Cadence-lypso, especially in the earlier years, can be considered pioneers, but the title of legend should be reserved for the one who created this unchanging quality in Creole music – the ones who directed its creation. I should state for the record that Gordon's legacy created Exile One, because he existed before Exile One.

In fact, the creation of the band and Cadence-Lypso happened over four (4) years (1973 to about 1977/78). Before that, Gordon had already ventured out on an extra- ordinary solo journey, one where the intellect of music and academia were his main pursuits (and he has been quite successful). So, while Exile One and Cadence-Lypso are important chapters in the Gordon Henderson's book, they are certainly not the book. Gordon is the legend and the music and band are acts of the legend; part of his lasting legacy. I felt it necessary to use Gordon as an example to place this in context, especially since I have been documenting his life for decades now. But that is another book, for another time, so let's go back to Eugenia: she certainly was an historic pioneering Dominican woman, especially when it comes to work and achievements in politics, but other women became lawyers and Prime Ministers as well. With the understanding that a lasting legacy is generally unalterable, here are the areas where I believe Dame Mary Eugenia Charles has attained some sort of notoriety which could count towards her legacy: Dame Eugenia rekindled – and some say, shifted – the spirit of the nation with her conservative views on enterprise development. It was under her reign that Dominica experienced a noticeable growth in industrial corporations, and the idea of corporatism as a means of political achievement also took root.

This was achieved on the heels a dismantled workers union sector, the cornerstone of the liberal political ideology which Eugenia opposed. Union leaders who once championed the cause of the 'little man' were accommodated mainly because of the anti-John coalition which swept through Dominica. Then again, this was not unilaterally the work of Eugenia; the entire nation – it seems – was up in arms against John's purported ills. Her Dominica Freedom Party was however the main beneficiary of the political switch, and Eugenia played her cards right. In fact, I believe she once famously said that the cards were in her hands. Former supporters of Patrick John, children of key union leaders and acolytes of the anti-John coalition were gifted with state amenities, including the issuance of one-way tickets out of Dominica, or want for a better term, indefinite scholarships to study abroad. I refer to this amazing political shift as a well-executed political realignment, and Eugenia must at least be credited for this. The shift from Democratic liberalism to a more conservative principle of governance created this new broader reality of trickled down economics – a popular conservative phrase which was popularized by United States President, Ronald Wilson Reagan. President Reagan was a leading patriarch of the neoconservative movement, and chief patron of transnational capitalism.

Dame Eugenia who once famously shared the stage with Reagan during the American military intervention in the 1983 Grenadian political impasse, was the queen of Caribbean conservatism, and she used capitalism to institute the realignment of Dominican politics. A new capitalist order was born, and the business savvy and ruling elites would be the major benefactors. So, not only did the elites influence political control, but the societal shift also granted them economic control.

It was during Eugenia's reign that most of the successful entrepreneurs gained firm grip on economic power. Before that and for some time during the 80s, Dominica's economy was driven largely by agriculture, and the people who owned the agricultural businesses, benefited most from, and drove the economy. Water was liquid crystal, agriculture was king, and banana was 'Green Gold' as Alwin Bully eloquently stated in his radio documentary. Farmers and rural citizens were thriving home-grown, walking enterprises, the small business sector, art, artists and musicians (who around the mid to late 1970s had already laid down a clear path to prosperity through music), arts and culture, and other indigenous enterprises like Kalinago craft, thrived on the solid foundation which the 1960s Edward Oliver Leblanc's Dominica Cultural Renaissance provided.

We will discuss the work of Leblanc, and Patrick John who succeeded him as political leader of Dominica in a follow-up stand-alone publication, but the fact that Eugenia was able to alter the fortunes of distinct Dominican groups of people with a dramatic modulation of the strata, dragged the names of her two predecessors in this publication. So, Dame Eugenia's 'legacy' is planted in the socio-political, cultural and economic realignment which occurred in Dominica under her tenure as Prime Minister, but this 'legacy' is not very clearly defined, as it does not necessarily satisfy my third thesis.

Her work can indeed be reformed, but with the present state of transnational capitalism, it would take an improbable calculation to redefine Dominica's and the global capitalist interests and influence. If some other leader is able to spearhead the reversal of the Dominica economic and political equation, it would have to be, for them, a proud achievement. Another of Eugenia's 'legacy' has to be her influence over, and the role she played in establishing a Dominican governing coalition in 2000. She brought people from two contrasting ideologies together: Liberals and Conservatives. But not only did Dame Eugenia succeed in bringing the sides together, she was able to engage with an individual whom she once discarded as 'communists, Roosevelt 'Rosie' Douglas, a self-declared leftist, to lead the Dominican government of 2000.

The legacy item vaguely satisfies all the benchmarks: the governing coalition which began with the Dame, when she famously said, "take them out at all cost" – referring to the United Workers Party (UWP)-led government, still costs the nation dearly, twenty-three years after. Initially, the coalition comprise the DLP and DFP, with Rosie Douglas leading this coalition as Prime Minister.
The coalition stretched to include members of the UWP,

in the persons of Julius Timothy (a UWP Founder), Loreen Bannis-Roberts (a former UWP Member of Parliament for Castle Bruce) and later, Shanks Esprit and Joseph Isaac – former UWP senator and Member of Parliament for Roseau, respectively. Other noteworthy UWP members followed the excursion towards the ruling coalition which has now (by 2022) been branded DLP, but it was Dame Eugenia's genius which initially sparked the power creation/sharing apparatus. At least for now, Eugenia's legacy is defined by this amazing feat of erasing the ideological divide in the Dominican political system, where today the Head of State of a left-of-center DLP government is a former leader of the conservative, or right-of-center party.

The government is also led by a 'conservative' Prime Minister – Roosevelt Skerrit – who replaced two leftist Prime Ministers – Pierre Charles and Rosie Douglas – who died in quick succession while serving in the Office of Prime Minister of the Commonwealth of Dominica.

The death of those two leaders are not linked to Eugenia's legacy, but they form part of the story.
This sort of political ideological reshuffling has not been known to have happened in quite the same way in any other political system. As significant or remarkable as this is, this cannot be said to be a clearly defined and lasting legacy in keeping with this book's benchmark. Chances are, someone could emerge and spearhead the realignment of Dominica's political ideologies to reflect a different power dynamic.

As unassailable as it now seems, nothing says this cannot be altered, modified or be totally reformed. There are several government policies which can be sighted, some of which individuals may even claim be Eugenia's legacy, but standard administrative policies like building of bridges, resurfacing roads, enhancing education, security and healthcare, procuring literacy, building houses, paying wages and salaries and the like, cannot be regarded as acts which define a leader's legacy. The truth is, another leader or government can also change this, and governments by their very nature – are expected to perform these basic functions. There will be an opportunity to extend the conversation in book two of Dominica Political Leadership Legacy Series (DPLLS) which will feature Patrick John.

As a standard disclaimer, this discussion on the achievements of Dame Eugenia is by no means complete. I deliberately left out those other achievements like her scholarship fund (foundation), the many accolades she received, and her good gestures which do not necessarily impact the whole of humanity in any profound way. With everything that has been stated, it is clear the Dame Eugenia is in a class by herself, and the contemporary breed of Caribbean politicians stand to learn a lot from her life, work and time. Eugenia represents an important link in the chain of Caribbean politics which saw ethics, principles, fair play and clear-cut ideologies as a means to effective leadership and tools to obtaining authority. Charles did not seek to degrade, instead she used her political savvy to great effect, and beneath her sometimes-aloof demeanor, there was a warm, introvert and caring lady who used her titles as robust shields to the fragility of femininity which had characterized life for Eugenia in a Caribbean, and the wider world.

Remembering the Dame

Much has been written about Dame Mary Eugenia Charles often compared to Margaret Thatcher as a second iron lady even if Thatcher preceded Charles by Just a few months in 1979 followed by Charles in 1980.

Dame Eugenia Charles was no copycat.

Historians are forced to be subjective for numerous reasons, so "readers" are also forced to interpret events of the past based on how the stories are told. This exercise could have been titled "from the horse's mouth". This interview which is a part of a series allows us to listen to and read a candid exchange between a young broadcaster working within the context of a radio feature titled "One hundred great Dominicans".

I feel privileged to invite you to indulge in this work because of my unique position of having been myself featured on this programme, having known Alex Bruno the interviewer for many years, having done business with Eugenia Charles' father whom she speaks so fondly and proudly of, and my personal contacts with the Dame. I first met Alex Bruno in the late eighties or probably early seventies in his office near the Canefield airport in

Dominica where he worked as an executive with a small airline company.

He was accompanied by his business partner and obvious close friend Val Cuffy a young pharmacist. These ambitious young men were interested in investing in the entertainment industry. From then I watched them grow. Alex grew to the point of building a multi-faceted career in communications including theatre, singer, songwriter among others and as I write became a university lecturer on the eve of his PhD in political science. I followed his progress from near and far.

When I read and listened to Alex Bruno's interview with Dame Eugenia Charles speaking of her father, I remembered as a young man walking into his bank with no account requesting a loan to travel to Guadeloupe to purchase musical instruments for a band. Even today in 2022, financial institutions in Dominica still look to music activity with a certain type of colonial contempt and condescension in which musicians and artists in general have a hard time doing financial business with banks. J B Charles: A man ahead of his time!

Mr. Charles expressed no ridicule and proved himself to be a singular innovator. My meeting with Mr. J B Charles was successful.

He examined my succinct and comprehensive business plan. He approved the loan; we shook hands and I later paid it off. This makes Mr. J B Charles a visionary in my mind which has led me to endorse and corroborate everything that Dame Eugenia said about her father in this interview. How I wish Alex Bruno could have interviewed the father! I first met the Dame in 1979 when I was the interim manager of DBS, Dominica's national broadcasting radio station.

It was a challenging period in the country's history for a hurricane David which demolished almost everything standing on the island, but worst of all in addition the country was traversing serious political turmoil because of a violent change of government which demanded immediate elections aimed mainly to somewhat restore political legitimacy.
The move from the established government to the interim has been referred to as a "parliamentary coup" among other euphemisms.

Dame Eugenia Charles who was the leader of the Freedom Party aided by a civil service union leader named Charles Savarin now President of the Commonwealth of Dominica, quite logically they did all in their power to take control of the only radio on island, DBS at such a crucial moment of electoral campaign. Or, at least to have as much presence as possible… It went as far as the union dragging me personally before the court for calling the police to take away workers who threw a

"sit in" organised by the union.

Dame Eugenia was the lawyer who represented the union in court and lost that case when she was choked by my defence. The details of this case carry significant historical importance that has been often overlooked. DBS radio is owned by the government of Dominica but the employees are not "civil servants".

The boss of the Civil Service Association (CSA) was Charles Savarin whom I have known way back from his school days when the secondary school boys of the day from Portsmouth assembled frequently at Benjamin's Park conversing with exclamations such as "exactly!" as they expressed their elitism. As a younger boy, I was much impressed. Those who knew Savarin from these days could not have been surprised by his oratory when as General Secretary of the CSA, he spoke his way to mobilising the entire country which led to the closure of services and a government overthrow.

It is this omnipotent Charles Savarin, much more popular than Dame Eugenia at the time, who approached me the then manager of DBS using a mixture of cunning and great negotiation skills to achieve something that was denied before by previous managers. He explained that the employees of DBS were not blessed with their workers' rights to be unionised and that as the person who wrote lyrics such as for the song "travay pou ayen", I should sign the agreement permitting DBS employees to become members of the CSA. I signed and the very next day, the employees in the vast majority came in and sat around refusing to be engaged in any work as a measure if industrial action. The idea was meant to stop all broadcasts. With the help of a tiny minority from inside and a few from outside, the station remained on air.

When the "sit in" had become an obvious failure, the strike or whatever manifestation was beefed-up to become a major festive party-like activity muscled-up to interrupt the broadcast. This was when I called the police who came and physically moved the strikers, protesters or whatever these employees called themselves. Soon after, a senior police officer came to my office politely inviting me to a court already in session. I was never summoned but the court was within walking distance. I was ushered directly to the witness stand amid a full house of cheering union members. I had absolutely no idea why I was almost dragged before the court. Miss Charles as the Dame was then called asked me a few routine questions like my name and position at the radio, job description, then, "why did you call the police...?" I responded, "because I considered it a siege."

"A siege?" she gasped with obvious surprise, "why didn't you say so?"

"This is exactly what I told the police who came, witnessed and acted accordingly", I replied.

The magistrate immediately dismissed the case. Strangely, weeks later, when she won the elections, she called me at the radio station with an offer. She seemed sad when I told her that her call was on the eve of my departure.

This may be the reflection of one aspect of her character. Six years later, I was placed next to her at an official event in Martinique and she expressed great pride in what I did then in promoting Dominica with my music. It is therefore with my experience of interaction with the various personalities in this document that I urge everyone to listen to and read the words of one of the most intriguing figures of the 20th century.

Gordon Henderson

Afterword

Life is about stories and stories are built on experiences. The one who best controls the narratives – stories – of those experiences has the superior story, and this has been the story of the evolving Dominica society, politics and culture. Irving Andre captures it best in his 2020 essay, The War on 'Dreads in Dominica: From Democracy to Papadocracy, in which he explains the intersection of the Dominican social phenomenon.

Grounding the shift in the Dominican consciousness within the ambits of the radical global movements of the 60s and 70s, Adre expresses that the academic, intellectual, cultural, social, spiritual, economic, political, and philosophical axis of the of a determined Dominican youths, hit an unavoidable crescendo that seriously threatened the entire Dominican status quo.

The Dreads, Andre argued, served as a metaphor for the underlying Dominican spirit that had been buried beneath the piles of unspoken and unsettled Dominica narratives which dates back to Africans who valiantly resisted the social order. Dominica is a more complex society than meets the eye. It is said that Barbados is exquisite, and if that be the case, Dominica is; absolutely exquisite. I say so because of the rugged nature of the island's history –

as rugged as her geographical terrain – and the splendor of the same ruggedness which Dominica is famous for. The interview with Dame Eugenia, which was one in a lifetime, revealed that much to me. Though an entire generation of Dominicans would have missed this interview in real time, this is as good a time as any for its release. For me, this interview was an overcompensation for a rookie broadcaster, and I thank the Dame for her wisdom and the willingness to share.

Dame Eugenia represented a particular ilk within the Dominican power structure, but she was not the entire power structure, and her views did not always represent those of the ruling class. In fact, the Dame was more misunderstood than she was understood, and her work and mission might have been maligned, or over shadowed, by her bullish conservative partisan ideology.

It is also true that Dame Eugenia had no illusion of becoming the last strong super authoritarian leader of Dominica; she simply wanted to play a small role in the development of her country, and that is what she did. Dame Eugenia was an unapologetic conservative, but that was when political ideologies meant something in Dominica and perhaps the world by extension.

It is not fair, therefore, to condemn her on the altar of left vs right politics, but instead, we can learn a lot from the Dame. Today, just as I felt twenty-four years ago when this interview was recorded, I believe that this message is timely and timeless. I am sorry to have held back this interview for nearly a quarter century, but I needed to pick the correct time when the Dominican, Caribbean and global community would need it most. Now is that time.

I am pleased to have respected the Dame's wish, not to have her story released as part of the 'One Hundred Great Dominicans' feature alongside the name of Patrick John. She did not, however, say that the interview should not be released at all. So, I have released it. In keeping with the Dame's passion, her life and work, one percent of the net proceeds from the sale of this book – for the next 99 years, will go towards a fund which has been established to assist with funding for students who are qualified and interested in the study of law, political science and/or history.

This is crucial, because of the colossal lack of political and civic knowledge among the Dominican populace. Most importantly, it is my wish that emerging generations will appreciate this work, and do all in their power to 'restore' Dominica to the majestic status as the Nature Island of the Caribbean which the island was endowed by the creator to be. I say this with some degree of reservation, because if we fail to come together as the Dame advised, two and more generations of Dominica down the road, the country could be faced with dire and probably irreparable social, cultural and political consequences.

My trust in the present generation gives me confidence in the future. We have not been able to work with a harmonized plan to enhance our nation since independence, 44 years ago, but I remain optimistic, although our partisan ambitions and national priorities are woefully unaligned. I hope that the political state of affairs will somehow be worked out in the interest of our people and the nation. Dame Eugenia relinquished her hold on power towards the end of the DFP's third consecutive term as the majority party in the government of Dominica.

Never would she seek to overstay her welcome in power. In fact, the Dame Eugenia I knew would see prolonged incumbency as an unhealthy act of political power-hugging. Alas, she was a leading accomplish to the creation of what clearly appears to be political power-hugging.

Eugenia certainly played a major role in instituting the power-sharing coalition between her Dominica FreedomParty (DFP) and arch political rival – the Dominica Labour Party (DLP) in 1999/2000.

Though that arrangement has since been realigned and certainly re-imagined to the point that the Dame herself would no longer recognize, this power-sharing arrangement has governed her beloved Dominica since. It is hoped that her words in this book could help to dismantle it.

Postscript

Eugenia was an unapologetic conservative who served in government during an era when governance was based on ideology. Apart from that, however, she placed her own stamp on political leadership, even if she was named 'The Iron Lady'; a title she shared with Margaret Thatcher, her British compatriot.

Eugenia's time in politics was marked by an element of recovering and realignment: recovery in the sense that Dominica and the region had bounced back from decades of economic challenges, and realignment in the sense that her reign saw a shift in the power balance of Dominica. As was captured in this book, Eugenia was a political hardliner whose work and actions continue to impact Dominica today. My hope is that, we can continue to analyze Eugenia's contribution, and I lament the failure to mark her 100th birthday with a series of initiatives.
I must confess that it was not for lack of trying on my part, but the system seemed detached from the not-too-distant past in a way that gave me much cause for concern.

This book, and others to follow in the Dominica Political Leadership Legacy Series (DPLLS), intends to reverse the tides of abandonment of our political history, which appears to be a staple of Dominica's politics. It is important that we learn from the past, lest we repeat old mistakes. Eugenia's work is, therefore, being kept alive through her own spoken words.

Eugenia was a founding member of the Dominica Freedom party which led the Government of Dominica from 21st July 1980 until 14th June 1995.

She served as Dominica's First Female Prime Minister during that period; adding to her record as Dominica's first female attorney-at-law. She was born on May 15, 1919 in the village of Pointe Michel in Dominica, and died on September 6, 2005 in Fort-de-France, Martinique.

Acknowledgment

Many have helped to steer me in the right direction, but my mother – the last of my parents – tops them all. Let me, therefore, acknowledge mammy for spearheading efforts to keep me grounded, and for the heartfelt comfort which she has offered me throughout my life.

As pertains to this particular project, Tamasha Toussaint deserves priority mention. She invested tremendous equity in transcribing this interview.
Nichole Georges-Bennett and Gordon Henderson also played pivotal roles in preparing the interview for publication, with Gordon contributing the foreword and a memory piece.

I express my profound gratitude to Sam George who designed this book and literally held my hand and walked me through the process of this, my very first publication. I shall forever be grateful.

My daughter, Anaya, added invaluable insight which have made me a 'younger' writer, and extended the reach of this book.

Let me convey my thank to Well Done Janitorial Services, LLC for sponsoring my book tour.

About the author

Alex Bruno has a vast array of accomplishments which complement his natural abilities and acquired skills. In addition to his experience as a broadcaster, playwright, communications professional, and entrepreneur. Alex, who is currently an Associate Professor of political science, is a well-known academic with special interests in Caribbean identities, political cultures, and institutions.

Alex earned a Bachelor's Degree in Philosophy with a minor in Theatre, and a Master's Degree in Political Science from Florida Atlantic University (FAU), and completed a second Master's Degree in International Relations (Studies) with a focus on Global Institutions at Florida International University's (FIU).

The thesis for the second MA: International Financial Institutions and Caribbean Development: A Comparison of Haiti & Jamaica, examines and discusses the impact of International Monetary Fund (IMF) and World Bank (WB) policies on the United Nations Development Program (UNDP) measurements in Haiti and Jamaica. The thesis explained the difficulties of those nations attaining the United Nation's Millennium Development Goals (MDGs).

This ties into Bruno's interest in studying the Caribbean region in line with the identities of the peoples of the Caribbean. Alex presented a public lecture on his research, Calypso & Soca: the Journey of Two Musical Genres in Dominic, at the University of the West Indies, Open Campus – Dominica, on February 14, 2014.

He also lectured on his research findings as follows: Mandela, Marley, Garvey and King: Four Different Voices, One Main Cause: Philosophical Concepts of Equal Rights which transcends all Boarders; at Florida Atlantic University in 2014, and the Concept of the American Dream: its epistemology and propensity for continuance as a metaphor for the unique American sovereign principle.

The latter was presented on September 13, 2011 at Florida Atlantic University's House Chambers in Boca Raton, Florida. Bruno also researched and presented a public Lecture on - The Philosophy of Livity and the Key to Longevity: The Dominican Centenarian Perspective. The presentation was given at the University of the West Indies (Dominica Open Campus) on November 5 -7, 2009.

Though this is Alex's first book, he has written several essays, poems, short stories, plays, skits, blog posts, articles, speeches and other such journals over the past three decades. Part of the author's motto is that he 'lives to write and writes to live', and readers will get a bit more of the passion which Bruno has put into his literary works. Professor Bruno, who is on the eve of completing his doctoral degree, is well placed to author this book. Dear reader, you are welcome to share the experience. Please engage with the material and feel free to share your views and reviews as they may impact the remaining books in the Dominica Political Leadership Legacy Series (DPLLS).

The second book, **'Patrick John - The Man'**, features Dominica's First Prime Minister, Patrick John. The third book, **'In Between Death'**, captures the work and 'legacies' of Rosie Douglas and Pierre Charles, Dominica's 4th and 5th Prime Ministers who both died, back-to-back while serving in office in October 2000 and January 2004, respectively. The fourth book in the series, **'Father of the Nation'** is an expose on Edward Oliver Leblanc – Dominica's First Premiere, and Mr. Edison James is featured in the fifth book – **'From Crisis to Recovery'**. The final book, **'Roosevelt Skerrit: Six in a Row'** covers Dominica's sixth Prime Minister Roosevelt Skerrit, and closes the DPLLS.

Copyright Permissions

About The Dame
by Dr. Lennox Honychurch
www.lennoxhonychurch.com

Explanatory Notes

On pages 69 through 71, when Dame Eugenia spoke about her great dislike for Patrick John, she was referring to 'Operation Red Dog' which was a military plot that was led by Klansman, Mike Perdue, and directed by Wolfgang Droege – a notorious Nazi – to seize control of Dominica in 1981.

Perdue was a disgraced former US Marine and truck driver who resided in Houston, Texas. Droege was Canadian. The plan of these Nazi and Klan mercenaries was to turn Dominica into an Aryan paradise to fund the Klan's operations. Dominica would also serve as a military training camp for mercenaries who had direct connection to the then Apartheid regime in South Africa. According to Stewart Bell, author of 'Bayou of Pigs', Patrick John along with, Wolfgang Droege, Don Black, Mike Perdue, Sydney Burnett-Alleyne, and James Alexander McQuirter were the chief planners of the operation. As a side note, readers will hear Patrick John's version of events surrounding the failed invasion in book two of the DPLLS: Patrick John: The Man.

On pages 95 and 96, when Dame Eugenia speaks of her government's relationship or partnership with France, and how she was able to secure financing for Dominica's road renovation project the name of the man whom she met with is most likely Claude Cheysson, the then Minister of External Relations or Foreign Affairs (1981–1984).

When Dame Eugenia blamed Edison James, the then Opposition Leader, for Dominica not having an international airport on pages 154 and 155, she was referring to a letter which wrote to the United States Department of State, on February 7, 1990, expressing concern about election interference.

In 2017, Prime Minister Roosevelt Skerrit cited James's letter as evidence that James was the reason Dominica does not have an international airport. I explore these accusations with Edison of in book four of the DPLLS: Edison James: From Crisis to Recovery.

Future Titles

- Patrick John: The Man

- In Between Death: The Douglas/Charles Legacy

- E. O. LeBlanc: Father of the Nation

- Edison James: From Crisis to Recovery

- Roosevelt Skerrit: Six in a Row